Competitors and Comrades

Competitors and Comrades

Culture, Economics, and Personality

Robert D. Smither

PRAEGER

PRAEGER SPECIAL STUDIES • PRAEGER SCIENTIFIC

New York • Philadelphia • Eastbourne, UK
Toronto • Hong Kong • Tokyo • Sydney

Library of Congress Cataloging in Publication Data

Smither, Robert D.
  Competitors and comrades.

  Bibliography: p.
  Includes index.
    1. Economics—Psychological aspects. 2. Comparative
economics. 3. Capitalism—Psychological aspects.
4. Communism and psychology. 5. Personality and
culture. I. Title.
HB74.P8S55   1984   155.9′2   84-15155
ISBN 0-03-001244-9 (alk. paper)

Published in 1984 by Praeger Publishers
CBS Educational and Professional Publishing,
a Division of CBS Inc.
521 Fifth Avenue, New York, NY 10175 USA

456789 052 987654321

Printed in the United States of America
on acid-free paper

To all the refugees

Foreword

As the graduate schools in our major research universities become increasingly more professional and specialized, more and more time is spent on research methods and less and less time is spent on education. Graduate training as opposed to graduate education has become the norm.

The physical sciences are ahistorical and, in a real sense, knowledge of the physical world is self-erasing. New knowledge literally displaces old knowledge and history becomes bunk. The humanities are largely history—there is typically no new knowledge, just new interpretations of old knowledge. In the cases of the physical sciences and the humanities, therefore, the emphasis on methodology over education probably has no serious consequences for the constituent disciplines.

The social sciences, however, exist somewhere between physics and literary criticism. They are, on the one hand, empirical but, on the other hand, the subject matter is historically situated in a way that physics will never be. Consequently, research in the social sciences is, alas, often politically inspired. That social science research may have ideological roots (for example, Cyril Burt's studies of the genetics of IQ) is in itself not necessarily a cause for alarm. What is alarming, however, are the consequences of current trends in graduate education. By focusing on methodology, on contemporary research, and on the exigencies of publication, we ignore the historical and philosophical roots of our disciplines and we increase our students' vulnerability to ideological biases. But then we come to the book at hand, Competitors and Comrades, and this short, clearly-written, and marvelously well-organized book provides a welcome and necessary antidote for ideology.

Personality psychology concerns the nature of human nature. As such it is a core topic for all the social sciences. At some point scholars in every field from political science to criminology must appeal to notions regarding human nature to explain their data. Personality psychology, in a very self-conscious way, takes human nature as its subject matter. Two obvious consequences follow from this. On the one hand, this means that personality theory is, by definition, an interdisciplinary topic, while on the other, this means that personality theory may be more liable to ideological intrusions than any other portion of psychology.

In this book, Robert Smither approaches the topic of personality theory from the detached perspective of the sociology of knowledge. He traces the development, over time, of views of human nature in the Soviet Union and the United States. By proceeding in this way he accomplishes a number of goals simultaneously. First, the book is a lively but at the same time scholarly overview of personality theory. As such it can be read for entertainment or profit by anyone seeking an accessible introduction to this fascinating and important subject matter.

Second, Smither carefully lays bare the ideological commitments entailed by the various perspectives on human nature. He does this by tracing the evolution of the capitalist character from Adam Smith to EST and transcendental meditation. At the same time, he describes the evolution of the socialist character from Hegel to modern Yugoslavia. This historical development of the subject matter is guaranteed to raise anyone's consciousness regarding the many connections between politics and the human sciences.

Third, Smither shows very clearly just how deeply critical of all forms of social organization Freud was and psychoanalysis remains. The conservatism of psychoanalysis provides a crucial vantage point from which to evaluate the progressive claims of both capitalism and communism. Although Smither labels Freud nihilistic (with some justification, of course), he clearly respects Freud's detachment from, and even hostility to, all forms of political engagement.

It is hard to think of anyone in the social sciences who would not profit from reading this book—it carries important information for both students and scholars, for political scientists and economists, for historians and sociologists. The lively style and broad perspective make this book interdisciplinary writing at its best.

Robert Hogan
Tulsa, Oklahoma

Preface

The idea for this book came from my experiences with refugee resettlement when I worked for the Indochinese Training Project in San Francisco and for the Cuban-Haitian Task Force and Office of Refugee Resettlement in Washington, D.C. In these jobs I dealt with hundreds of resettlement workers and refugees across a wide variety of situations: a former general who was a typist in a camera shop, an ex-ambassador working as a thrift-shop cashier, farmers unfamiliar with pencils, voodoo cultists seeking political asylum, college students who believed that Haile Selassie and his dog had the ability to become invisible, and people who believed that blacks were still slaves in the United States.

The majority of refugees were people who, for whatever reasons, had been forced to leave their own countries and to start new lives in the United States. In varying degrees, the backgrounds of these people either helped or hindered their adjustments to life in American society. The refugees all faced the tasks of finding homes, jobs, and schools, and becoming productive tax-paying members of a system they often knew little about. In addition, they were expected to refrain from any public expression of their old ways of life—like the practice of voodoo—that did not fit in with American culture.

One comment I often heard from the resettlement workers who had the job of helping these people through the transition from refugee to self-supporting resident or citizen was that most refugees from socialist societies were extremely difficult to resettle in the United States. These people did not know or seem to be able to understand the basic rules of the capitalist system under which the United States operates. While the U.S. government expected the refugees to find a place to live, learn English, get a job, stop receiving welfare, and become independent as soon as possible, the intentions of the refugees were often quite different.

In any group of refugees from socialist states, there were always a substantial number who, regardless of social background, did not mind being dependent upon the government and who apparently had no intentions of trying to make it on their own. According to the popular wisdom of the resettlement workers, refugees from socialist countries almost invariably expected the U.S. government to be as beneficent as socialist governments in providing jobs, housing, transportation, social services, and other necessities of life.

Although such generalizations do not hold true in every case, resettlement workers professing this view seemed to have an impressive body of anecdotal evidence about the difficulties of resettling individuals from socialist states. One famous episode concerned a family of Soviet refugees resettled to Los Angeles by the U.S. Catholic Conference. The Catholic Conference is a multimillion dollar charity operation that resettles over 50 percent of the refugees, regardless of faith, who come to the United States. U.S.C.C. resettled the Soviet family into a small apartment that had adequate, but obviously second-hand furniture. A few days after their arrival, the family went back to the resettlement office to demand new furniture; the puzzled social service workers told them that new furniture was out of the question. Some months later the family returned with their unmarried teenage daughter, now pregnant. They asked the Catholic Conference to pay for an abortion and were amazed and indignant that the resettlement workers refused the request. Although they were well aware of the Church's attitude toward abortion, the refugees regarded abortion as a basic human right, and certainly one that should be available in a "free country" like the United States.

I often heard the same kind of complaints about Cuban refugees, particularly those who had come in the Mariel boatlift of 1980. Specifically, resettlement workers, and many other Cubans, believed that those who were born and grew up before the revolution were much easier to resettle than those who had grown up under Castro. (The Mariel group can hardly be considered a representative sample of all Cuban refugees, however, since there is strong evidence that many of the people that the Cuban government sent to the United States then came from jails and asylums.)

The Mariel Cubans did, in fact, seem to be considerably more demanding of social service providers than the Cuban groups that had come earlier. The Mariel Cubans frequently remarked that they did not have to take jobs they did not like since it was the obligation of any government, Cuban or American, to provide them with employment. They made extreme demands on service providers, then appeared to be almost entirely dependent on what those providers could give them. Resettlement workers often commented on the fact that the Mariel Cubans did not seem to appreciate that independence and self-reliance are positive values in the American system, that taking handouts is not, and that they were expected to learn to behave in accordance with those values.

Sometimes this misunderstanding of what kinds of behaviors are acceptable to Americans took on a more unusual aspect. One of the major voluntary agencies involved with resettlement sponsored ten homosexual Cubans to their branch office in Philadelphia. During the time that the ten were in flight from Miami, they changed from male attire to female. They teased their hair and did their fingernails. The voluntary agency officials awaiting at the airport were shocked to find that the ten males they had sponsored had arrived "in drag." When the counselors told the refugees that such behavior is not acceptable in the United States, or at least not quite so openly, the refugees replied that the United States is a free country—unlike Cuba—and consequently they could dress any way they liked. After several days of unsuccessful job-hunting, however, most of the Cubans stopped wearing female clothing in public—but they refused for a long time to give up their fingernail polish.

This book is about the different ideas of human nature that are found in capitalist and socialist societies such as the United States and the Soviet Union, how our ideas about human nature simply reflect the economic culture in which we were raised, and how difficult it is to go from one culture to another. Throughout this book, the experience of the refugee—the person who has learned to act appropriately in one culture, then is faced with learning a new set of appropriate behaviors—is used to illustrate the strength of the factor that is clearly the greatest determinant of personality and behavior—economics.

Contents

Competitors and Comrades

1

The Importance of Conformity

In any culture, individuals learn from birth what kinds of behavior are going to be acceptable to the other people around them. A baby finds out quickly what pleases mother, what annoys her, what gets rewarded by food, attention, a smile, or whatever pleases the baby, and also what leads to punishment. What determines the behaviors that the mother—then the father, teacher, friends, boss, husband, wife, and children—rewards is, first of all, the personality of the one doing the rewarding. What he or she rewards is what his or her own mother, father, teacher, etc., rewarded. These responses that we learn in early childhood constitute one important aspect of personality.

In a larger sense, however, the behaviors that people learn are the products of the value system of the society in which they live. If respect for tradition, ancestors, family, and religion are important, then people will learn to act in ways that reflect this value when dealing with parents, teachers, and other authorities. If, on the other hand, behaviors that show respect for science, technology, individual rights, and youth are rewarded, people will have a different style of behavior when dealing with authorities.

One of the clearest examples of culture's effect on ways of dealing with authority is the job interview. Americans use the job interview as an opportunity to talk about their accomplishments, demonstrate what likeable persons they are, and to tell potential employers what valuable additions they would be to their companies. Indochinese refugees unfamiliar with this particular rite of passage often react to this kind of behavior with horror. In an Indochinese setting, American job-interview behavior would be considered to be in extremely poor taste, and a behavior not very likely to be rewarded with a job offer. In Indochinese cultures it is usually more important to show respect

1

for the interviewer by submissive behavior, like averting one's eyes and acting deferential than to boast about one's abilities.

For an individual placed in a new culture, just as a child growing up, adaptation is a process of learning what behaviors are acceptable—i.e., get a favorable response—in the new culture. Just as "immature" behavior acceptable in high school is no longer acceptable in college, and Midwestern hospitality toward strangers doesn't always fare well in New York City, refugees discover that the behaviors they had learned in their own countries are not necessarily what will elicit favorable responses in the United States.

The greater the degree of a person's skill in judging the people around him, the faster he will discover what kinds of behavior are going to be rewarded. For most people, the process of maturation increases one's skills in identifying behaviors that bring favorable responses in different situations. For example, one's manner of behavior may differ greatly between the Saturday night date and the Sunday morning sermon, or in voicing one's opinion at home about working long hours versus one's opinion on that matter as expressed in front of one's boss. Different situations obviously call for different behaviors. In fact, maturity might be defined as knowing when to act how.

In the jargon of social science, these individual instances of behavior designed to elicit favorable—or in certain circumstances, unfavorable—responses from other people can be lumped together under the category of "roles." Roles are simply sequences of actions or behaviors that seem situationally appropriate to an individual. When dealing with other people, individuals adopt the "style" of response that they are comfortable with, as with a friend, or that they know is required by the situation, as in a job interview. In behavioral terms, the role that one adopts will determine the kinds of responses one makes to stimuli coming from the situation.

Individuals from other cultures, such as refugees, have learned roles that cover situations that occur in their lives in their own cultures, but they won't necessarily know the roles appropriate to American culture. Nevertheless, Americans expect refugees to learn quickly the roles that Americans find acceptable and to try to act, at least in public, like members of the majority culture. For example, since the majority of Americans profess to believe in democracy, progress, and the sanctity of the free enterprise system, roles that demonstrate a belief in those values are going to be responded to far more favorably than roles that demonstrate a willingness to stay on welfare, be overly modest in a job interview, or ask the Catholic Church to pay for an abortion.

When circumstances lead to an individual's learning roles that are not acceptable to society—such as "criminal," "drug addict," or "outcast"—the results can be quite tragic. Many of the problems of modern society are traceable to problems with the roles that people have learned. In his moving and eloquent example of the high cost of learning unacceptable roles, psychoanalyst Erik Erikson has written about the plight of the Sioux Indians in modern America. The Sioux were once proud and fierce warriors, roaming across the plains in pursuit of buffalo and booty from raids upon their neighbors. Their culture required a strict cooperation within the tribe and an unrelenting fierceness in battle. Starting from a psychoanalytic frame of reference, Erikson described in some detail the child-rearing practices that shaped the behavior of the children so that they grew up to be gentle and cooperative with their own people and fearless when dealing with outsiders.

Specifically, Sioux mothers were extremely lenient when it came to toilet training and breast-feeding, but somewhat punishing when the nursing babies, as a natural result of the teething process, would bite their mothers' breasts. According to Erikson, the babies were kept on a cardleboard that allowed no free movement. When the babies would bite their mothers' breasts, the mothers would thump the children on the forehead. This practice led to a furious reaction on the part of the babies, but being tightly strapped to the cradleboard, the babies had no way of expressing that rage. Erikson suggested that the unexpressed rage of childhood, traceable to this and other child-rearing practices, is what made the Sioux Indians such successful warriors. One of the major problems with the Sioux Indians, from a psychoanalytic viewpoint, is that cultural practices still raise children to be warriors. They know the behaviors that are appropriate to a society that no longer exists. Tied to the reservation, they have little opportunity to learn new behaviors or roles that fit in better with modern American culture.

In a similar study of the inappropriate roles that American Indians learn, anthropologist E. M. Bruner has described the dances of the Mandan-Hidatsu, in which the Indians give away their possessions. Indians who have learned something about Anglo-society know that such practices are not acceptable in modern America so they don't participate in the dances. Those who cling to the old ways of the tribe have no hope of making it in the Anglo-culture, but those who attempt to give up the past and learn the ways of the majority will also pay a heavy psychological price. Bruner described the problems of the marginal Indian families who seemed to be caught between two sets of roles:

> Observation indicates that members of the marginal families are restless, unsatisfied, rather unpredictable, and some are psychologically unstable. In every one of these families there is a constant pattern of excessive drinking and fighting, and every adult male has a jail record for committing minor offenses.

The more different cultures are, the more difference between roles individuals will adopt. Few of the roles and values of American Indian culture will lead to success in modern, corporate, technological America. Given the differences between the roles taught in capitalist and socialist systems, it is not surprising that the person who is raised to be a good socialist is probably going to encounter some problems succeeding in capitalist society.

This book starts with the simple premise that, as people grow, they learn roles appropriate to their environments, and the greater the difference between environments, the greater the difference in roles learned. Since the sum of an individual's roles is one way of describing personality, a socialist environment is going to give rise to a different kind of personality than a capitalist environment.

Interestingly, the critical importance of the economic system in personality development is generally unrecognized by psychologists. In the West, psychologists have generally looked to the three traditions of psychoanalysis, behaviorism, or existential/humanistic psychology to explain human nature, while Soviet psychologists have relied upon Marx, Pavlov, and Makarenko. All of these theories purport to be scientific explanations for personality. Yet if we look at the major theories of personality proposed by psychologists in either the capitalist United States or the socialist Soviet Union, we find that these "scientific" ideas, like our own personalities, are simply reflections of the economic culture in the country where the theory was developed.

2

The Validity of Stereotypes

Association with one another, theoretical work,
the struggle under a definite banner, collective
discipline, the hardening under fire of danger,
these things gradually shape the revolutionary
type. It would be perfectly natural to speak of the
psychological type of the Bolshevik, in contrast
for example, to that of the Menshevik. An eye
sufficiently experienced could tell a Bolshevik
from a Menshevik even by his outward appearance, with only a slight percentage of error.

Trotsky

Roles are behaviors that are combined in an organized fashion
to respond to specific situations. We learn these roles as we grow and
interact with a variety of people and try to elicit favorable responses
from them. As children we try all kinds of behaviors through play, but
as we mature we begin to recognize some kinds of roles as being more
comfortable to us than others. We tend to use these particular roles
more frequently over a wide variety of situations. Through the roles
that we adopt and use often we come to be known to others as "shy,"
"nice," "friendly," "manipulative," or any other personality descrip-
tor. As the mystic P. D. Ouspensky described the process:

Everybody has a certain number of roles: one corresponds
to one set of conditions, another to another and so on. Man
himself seldom notices these differences. For instance, he
has one role for his work, another for his home, yet another among friends, another if he is interested in sport,

5

and so on. These roles are easier to observe in other
people than in oneself.

Whereas we may occasionally show some flexibility in respond-
ing to specific situations with uncharacteristic behaviors, most of us
tend to adopt general patterns of role behaviors that we use throughout our lives. These general patterns are what we mean when we use
the terms personality or character.

Although we in the West are particularly inclined to believe that
we choose the roles that constitute our personalities, for most of us
it is the economic culture of society that determines the roles we use.
And since economic culture is a critical factor in all the components
that shape personality—including family structure, the varying ways
in which the different sexes and races are treated by society, the values taught in the educational system, the political and religious ideologies of the society, courtship and marriage practices, and the nature
of the work environment—people coming from different economic cultures are going to have different kinds of personalities. This is particularly true with regard to the socialist economic culture of the
Soviet Union and the capitalist economic culture of the United States.

GROUP DIFFERENCES AND SIMILARITIES

In spite of other differences, one way in which the systems of the
United States and the Soviet Union are quite similar is the clear dichotomy made between the roles of the sexes. In spite of rhetoric on both
sides and a few recent changes in the perception of sex roles, the social systems of both societies use biology, family structure, the educational system, religion, and the work environment to reward one
set of roles for males and another for females.

From early ages, males and females learn some similar, and
some completely distinct, roles. For example, the role of "breadwinner" in both societies is still much more likely to be reserved for
males, while "homemaker" or "supplemental income earner" is reserved for females. In spite of the "liberation" of women in both societies, working Soviet wives still do 60 to 70 percent of the housework,
and American men do, at the very most, only one-third of childcare
and household tasks. (Working American males of all educational levels resent being asked to do housework.) Sex differences, are of
course, not limited to the home: female attorneys in the United States
earn a median of $33,000 annually compared to the $53,000 that male
attorneys earn; working women in the United States earn on the average, 58 percent of the salaries of their male counterparts. Because
of this dichotomy in the sex roles in both cultures, male and female

capitalist and socialist personalities are going to have some differences.

Another consideration is the influence of the system on the personalities of members of minority cultures. Because minority cultures
are often quite different from the majority culture, minorities also
learn a different set of roles from the majority. (The Soviet Union,
for example, recognized 92 nationalities in the 1979 census, and Soviet
citizens are required to "choose" their nationalities at age 16 when the
internal passport is issued.) Since the institutions of the United States
and the Soviet Union are dominated by the majority culture, success
for minorities in the institutions of these societies tends to correlate
with how much they are willing to assume roles that the majority finds
acceptable.

An example of the power of the dominant group is evident in the
corporate suites of modern America, where the striking majority of
professionals are white, male, clean-shaven, married once and still
married, conservative in dress, and from a prestigious college. These
homogeneous individuals replace themselves with people like themselves: regardless of affirmative action and equal employment opportunity legislation, they generally try to avoid allowing women or minorities to reach positions of power.

Wilbert Moore has referred to these people at the top—who, like
it or not, have a tremendous influence over our lives—as a bureaucratic
kinship system based on homosexual reproduction. With relatively few
exceptions, blacks and women don't make it into the system simply
because they aren't sufficiently similar to those who operate the system. The women, blacks, and other minorities who do make it do so
mainly because they are able to play the roles that those at the top
reward.

This emphasis on homogeneity at the top is not limited to the
United States. Of the 13 members of the Politburo at the time of
Brezhnev, 8 were over 70 years old and 4 were over 60. On the average, each member had belonged to the Party for 47 years. Of the 13
members, 9 were ethnic Russians, and of the 4 minority members,
only 1 was from a non-European republic. Eight of the members had
technical training in areas such as economics, metallurgy, or engineering, and the remaining 5 had spent most of their careers as Party
functionaries. Thus, one could say that the life experiences of the people who had made it to the top in the Soviet Union were remarkably
similar. Since organizational psychology teaches us that leaders replace themselves with people like themselves, there was little reason
to expect much change in the Andropov-era Politburo—in spite of the
apochryphal stories about Andropov's reported fondness for Western
jazz and Scotch whiskey.

Given these considerations, when I refer to capitalist or socialist personality in this book, I am referring first of all to white American or Soviet males, white American or Soviet females to a lesser extent, and minorities only so far as they have adopted the roles of the majority.

DEVELOPING STEREOTYPES

Once while riding in the car with a Jewish friend, we heard on the radio that several members of an Italian family of trapeze artists had been killed during practice for the evening's performance of the circus. In spite of their personal tragedy, the remaining members of the family had vowed that "the show would go on" that night. My friend commented with some amusement that going on with the show was "so Christian." When I asked him what he meant, he expressed his view that Christians had a devotion to duty that bordered on the absurd, and that Catholics in particular seemed to appreciate opportunities to display their suffering. Although my friend would agree that this kind of cultural generalization is not true in every case, he was summarizing his views about a particular group by attributing to its members certain roles that he felt were characteristic of most Christians. ("All Jews are cynics," said a Catholic friend when I asked him about the meaning of my other friend's comments.)

In American social science literature since the 1940s, group stereotypes have been considered anathema to both science and humanism. Perhaps as a reaction to the extremely racist views of Germans and Japanese prevalent during World War II, individuals who relied upon stereotypes to characterize different groups were seen as conservative, backward, or racist. With the beginnings of the civil rights movement in the 1950s this view was reinforced: Western science tells us that everyone is unique and humanism mandates that we consider each person an individual.

Yet anyone who doesn't live in an ivory tower recognizes two facts about stereotypes. First, like it or not, they are often correct, and second, they are not necessarily unflattering. Stereotypes are simply summarizations of impressions about groups that we apply when we meet individuals whose behavior or personality is unknown to us. The danger of stereotypes, of course, is that they often become the sole reference point for judging others—we pay attention to details that confirm our ideas about specific groups and ignore those that contradict our prejudices.

Among the refugees and newcomers to the United States I have dealt with, certain stereotypes about Americans seemed universal. Americans are seen as being friendly and generous, on the one hand, but they tend to look at life in terms of business prospects and possessions on the other. Newly-arrived people from other cultures tend to believe that it is very easy to become rich in the United States, but also believe that this is a violent society where foreigners in particular have to be on guard against crime. Finally, however open and warm Americans may be toward strangers, they have very low standards of morality. Refugees tend to think that everyone in the United States is divorced, American women are "loose," and that American men are thoughtless and irresponsible when it comes to their families. People from other cultures are particularly puzzled with the way in which Americans seem to dislike or be angry with their parents, and they don't understand the American preoccupation with psychotherapy and counseling.

While some of these stereotypes are blatantly incorrect, it is not difficult to see how, from a given perspective, others might be perceived as being apt. But though they might be true in a general sense, they are certainly not always true in a specific sense, and it is on the invalidity of stereotypes that Western science has chosen to focus. Capitalist culture, for reasons to be discussed later, emphasizes a focus on the individual and generally eschews any sacrifice of individuality for group identity. Further, since Western psychology has been traditionally fixated on the individual rather than the group, the uniqueness of each individual is more valued than the similarities of individuals. Western personality theorists in particular are not as interested in how people are alike as how they are different. The similarities between the personalities of Lenin and Trotsky, for example, are not nearly so interesting as the piece of personality trivia alleging that although Lenin bought his suits off the rack, Trotsky preferred to have his clothes tailor-made.

However much social science objects to stereotyping, it is still something that everyone, including the social scientist, does. People hold opinions about the personalities of used car salesmen, accountants, and funeral directors just as they hold opinions about blacks, Jews, and WASPs. Often, when we discover that an individual belongs to a certain group, we begin to expect him or her to act in certain ways in certain situations. If we are sufficiently perceptive, we may be able to identify what group a person belongs to by his or her behavior or appearance, as in the case of the differences between Bolsheviks and Mensheviks that Trotsky described in the beginning of this chapter.

In this book I am dealing not so much with stereotypes as with what Erich Fromm has called the "social character"—the repertoire of roles that is shared by most members of the same culture. These roles are shaped within all members of a society so that a particular culture may survive. As Wilhelm Reich described the process:

Every social organization creates those character structures which it needs to exist. . . . It is not a matter of indoctrinating attitudes and opinions but of a far-reaching process in every new generation of a given society, the purpose of which is to effect a change in and mold psychic structures (and this in all layers of the population) in conformity with the social order.

The cultural influences that create the social character so important in the early years of our lives and that, for most of us, continue relatively unchanged throughout our lives, dramatically influence who we are and what we believe. Although psychotherapy or radical change in our lives may alter some of the roles we use, most of us do not have much say about who we are and what we currently believe. This is particularly true with regard to the values that come from the economic order into which we are born. As anthropologist Leslie White observed:

> People do not have communal or private systems of property because they want them or it is human nature to prefer one to the other. In a very realistic sense, they do not "have them" at all; rather <u>it is the cultures which possess the people who have been born into them</u>. Attitudes, sentiments, and behavior toward property are determined by the type of economic system into which one is born.

CHOOSING A THEORY OF PERSONALITY

Since the beginning of time, people have been wondering about the "true" nature of mankind. Is it good? Evil? Religious? Altruistic? Aggressive? Personality theory is the area of psychology that attempts to answer the same kinds of questions: What are people like? How did they get that way? How might they behave in the future? As a rule, most theories of personality also attempt to explain how people might be made "better."

Psychologist Gordon Allport stressed the importance of distinguishing between the two aspects of personality that he called the "nomothetic" and "idiographic." Nomothetic aspects of personality are widely distributed within populations, while idiographic aspects are particular to the individual. In this book, the term "personality" is used in its nomothetic sense and refers to the collections of behaviors that come from the roles that an individual has adopted throughout his or her life. This book does not propose a new theory of personality, but is rather an attempt to understand the differences in personality and behavior in people who are raised in capitalist systems and those raised in socialist systems. When we look at the psychological theories about human nature that prevail in these respective systems, it is striking how much Western views of human nature are coincident with capitalist views and Soviet views are coincident with Marxism. In spite of their professed adherence to the goals and practices of empirical science, most theories of personality are much more the products of the economic cultures of their originators than they are value-free descriptions of human nature.

Whereas Western psychologists are willing to consider personality as the result of parent-child interactions, genetic inheritance, libidinous drives, family structure, body type, or the drive to self-actualization, they have yet to acknowledge the importance of economic ideology on character formation. When Western psychologists do consider economics—as in the work of George Katona, for example—it is generally in the not surprising sense of the effect of psychology on economic behavior and consumerism. But with regard to human nature, this is looking at the problem backward, since it is economic ideology that determines, to a large extent, human behavior. Because economic ideology is such a powerful force in shaping any culture, there will never be an understanding of human nature without an understanding of the influence of economic ideology on the individual. Theories of personality that do not consider the effects of the economic environment in which people live are actually quite limited in their usefulness.

Whatever one's theoretical predilection in explaining personality, however, people in any society agree on certain basic expectations about the behavior of others: they expect people to behave consistently most of the time, and they will reward those roles that they find acceptable and ignore or punish those that they do not. And certainly the majority of people in any society want to see behaviors that fit into the range of acceptable roles in their own social character or culture. In the United States, people generally like to see roles that demonstrate hard work, consumption, and independence, and in the Soviet Union, people like to see roles that demonstrate a devotion to duty, sociability, and concern for one's comrades.

As in the case of the refugee, differences in roles between cultures becomes quite obvious when one has been raised to perform one way and suddenly is expected to perform another. Shortly after the eruption of Mt. Saint Helens in 1980, the Laotian community of San Francisco held a benefit for the victims of that disaster. The benefit was billed as an opportunity for the community to repay some of the kindness shown them by Americans. Staging fundraisers, however, is not a role widely taught in Laotian society. At the "Volcano Party," refugees served beef lemon grass and Lao vegetables along with Coca-Cola and Budweiser, Lao children performed traditional dances to the accompaniment of a Laotian rock-and-roll band that also played songs by Chuck Berry and the Beatles. Although the purpose of the party was to raise money for the disaster victims, one looked in vain for a place to make a donation. At the Volcano Party, Americans had the opportunity to experience that state of half-acculturation that most refugees experience to some degree throughout their lives. The Laotians had not been raised to be Americans, but they were doing their best to provide role behaviors that Americans would like.

Most people, including personality theorists, never think systematically about the broad differences between cultures, their effects on personality, or how difficult it must be to go from one set of roles to another. These differences in behavior start a long way back: for the society, from the philosophical arguments of some long-dead economic theorist. As social scientists and as ordinary people trying to understand other people, it is critical that we recognize the influence of economic culture on who we are and what we do.

3

The Capitalist Personality

> [Capitalism] is a truly moral science, the most
> moral of all sciences. Its principal thesis is the
> renunciation of life and of human needs. The less
> you eat, drink, buy books, go to the theatre or to
> balls, or to the public house, and the less you
> love, theorize, sing, paint, fence, etc., the more
> you will save and the greater will become your
> treasure which neither moth nor rust will cor-
> rupt—your capital.
>
> Marx

Shortly after the fall of Saigon I was assigned a client who appeared to be badly in need of a job. Mr. Nguyen was a former colonel
in the ARVN who was apparently accustomed to the better things in
life: he told me that even during the worst of the war he had a heli-
copter fly himself and his family to the beach every weekend. Now,
however, he appeared to be without any means of supporting himself
or his family except for the meager funds provided by the federal government for refugee relief.

In addition to his army duties, however, Mr. Nguyen had owned
a travel agency in Saigon. For weeks I tried to talk him into applying
for a job as a travel agent, and I even managed to arrange several
interviews. Mr. Nguyen, however, seemed resistant to going on these
interviews, and I attributed this reticence to the well-known Vietnamese aversion to American job interview behavior. After several frus-
trating weeks of working with Mr. Nguyen, I gave up on the case, fig-
uring that he would rather accept government support than find a job.
Some time later, however, I discovered that during this period Mr.

Nguyen had been driving a taxi and taking English lessons and had amassed enough capital to establish his own travel agency. To my chagrin, I also learned that he had bought a used BMW and even offered the head of our refugee resettlement agency a job working for him!

The case of Mr. Nguyen is a classic example of the success stories of immigrants who arrive to the United States without anything and make an amazing adaptation to the capitalist system. Capitalist theorists use examples such as Mr. Nguyen to illustrate the "rightness" of the capitalist system and as proof of its congruence with basic human nature.

Capitalist theorists write about the ultimate perfectability of man and how, if the world is not interfered with and people are allowed to pursue their natural wants, then everyone benefits. Capitalist theorists believe that people are at heart economic beings who can become satisfied materially and spiritually through their exchange—but only if that exchange is the result of hard work, the denial of unnecessary pleasures, preservation of the social order, and, above all, maintaining their liberty by keeping government out of their personal affairs.

If men—and, presumably, women—can be left to their own devices, free of the interference of the state, there will be economic abundance for all, political and social freedom, and a busy and productive world in which people pursue their natural motivation: the pleasure that economic satisfaction brings. Governmental meddling in the natural order of supply and demand, as well as attempts to deprive people of their major motivation—economic satisfaction through the accumulation of wealth—is the force that keeps people from realizing their true potentials.

THE CAPITALIST MYTH OF CREATION

According to anthropologist Marvin Harris, whose account of the rise of capitalism takes a materialist, rather than psychological perspective, capitalism is the natural product of the evolution of human culture. As populations continued to expand throughout prehistory, tools developed and societies began to codify their cultures and become states. In Western Europe, the Franks, Gauls, and Britons divided their societies into three hereditary castes which are the forerunners of the modern social classes: warriors (the aristocracy), priests, and commoners. Because the main preoccupation of these societies was war, greater physical strength gave males a privileged position that continues into modern times.

According to Harris, the population of England in 500 A.D. was estimated to have been 9 persons per square mile. However, 600 years later the population had more than tripled, with an estimated 30 persons per square mile (as opposed to 592 in 1983). As population increased, efficiency declined—farmers had to work harder to feed more people and more people meant less land to farm. Further, the lords began to seek greater profits and turned to sheep-raising rather than agriculture. The decline of land available for farming resulted in the pauperization of many farmers, who were forced to move to the towns to seek work.

In the middle of the fourteenth century, the Black Death killed up to one-half the population of Europe. Harris suggests that the high death rate is partly attributable to the decline in nutritional standards as land became less productive and people were forced to leave the estates for the towns. The sudden scarcity of labor resulting from the Black Death freed the commoners from the total domination by the lords, and a long period of intense social and political struggle began.

Modern social scientists are unclear about the linkage between the Reformation and the rise of capitalism, but they tend to agree about a linkage between the Reformation, Protestantism, and qualities of the capitalist personality. To summarize sociologist Max Weber's argument about the Reformation and Protestantism, the Protestant preoccupation with the accumulation of wealth is traceable to Luther's translation of Ecclesiastes 11:21, "Trust in the Lord and abide in thy calling." Luther was emphasizing the importance of the secular life, and particularly one's calling or occupation, and deemphasizing the role of the church.

The theologian John Calvin (1509-64) carried Luther's interpretation further, suggesting that first, life required the strictest discipline in order to avoid temptation and achieve salvation, and second, that work is the best prophylactic against temptation. Since it was money that often brought temptation, Calvin argued that wealth should be given to the church or spent on public welfare, but in no case used for extravagance or pleasure. Those who were going to heaven lived lives of asceticism and frugality, regardless of the amount of capital they had amassed. Those who had amassed capital were blessed by God, but any demonstration of profligacy or dissipation jeopardized their chances for an afterlife.

Luther believed that the natural state of man was agrarian-based: a simple kind of farm life that left little time for preoccupation with worldly affairs, but enough time for contemplation of God. Calvin, on the other hand, felt that industrial society offered the best opportunities for the growth of the church and consequently took an active interest in economic matters. He arranged for a loan to establish a velvet factory in Geneva to provide work for the poor, and he attempted to ban the playing-card industry in England. Calvin's asceticism was worldly—while he believed in hard work and deprivation, he also supported the use of money, credit, and usury. According to Calvin, when God read one's profit and loss statement on the day of judgment, there had better be a profit—or at least signs of a good effort—if one wanted to enter heaven.

However compelling Weber's thesis about Protestantism and capitalism, however, there are, of course, other sociological or historical interpretations for the rise of capitalism. The British economist R. H. Tawney has suggested that Catholicism held within itself the seeds of capitalism and that the Reformation simply speeded up a process already in progress. Another British economist, H. M. Robertson, has argued that capitalism was learned by the Crusaders from the Syrians and was facilitated in its development by Pisano's book on double entry bookkeeping in 1543. Whatever the impetus for capitalism, however, most social scientists agree that Protestantism was a strong force in fostering its growth.

HUMAN NATURE IN CAPITALIST THEORY

Whatever the cultural or sociological backgrounds for capitalism, the philosophical justification—the "proof" that capitalism is in order with the natural state of man—is generally attributed to the later works of Adam Smith (1723-90).

Smith held the chair of Moral Philosophy at the University of Glasgow and in 1776 published the book he is best known for, An Inquiry into the Nature and Causes of the Wealth of Nations.

In The Wealth of Nations, Smith brought the writings of earlier economic philosophers together in an incisive analysis of the state of the British economy and, at the same time, introduced a new conception of human nature. It is Smith's emphasis on man's egotism, self-interest, and need to barter that prevails in capitalist theory today. The Wealth of Nations is a broad and far-reaching work that only tangentially touches on matters relevant to personality theory, but underlying all the economic discussions are Smith's assumptions about the nature of man and his place in the natural order of things.

Smith was greatly influenced in his view of human nature by the British philosophers Thomas Hobbes (1588-1679) and John Locke (1632-1704). Hobbes had argued that when men lived in a state of nature, life was "solitary, poor, nasty, brutish, and short." Cooperation has never been a natural condition for men, Hobbes wrote, but is necessitated by the growth of population and the scarcity of resources. In order to assure the orderliness of society, men make convenants which, taken together, constitute government. The ultimate purpose of these governments, according to Hobbes, is to enhance individual advantages.

John Locke, whose writings on government greatly influenced Jefferson, Madison, and Hamilton, and whose other writings on the empirical method have virtually dominated the development of Western science, argued that man in his natural state is peaceful and is naturally endowed with the right to "life, liberty, and property." Whereas the church often stressed the superiority of communal ownership of property, it is private property that is natural to man. Governments, in Locke's view, exist solely to protect the rights of the individual and his property.

Smith accepted the prevailing views of Hobbes and Locke and used them to explain the phenomenon of the growth of the British economy, and in particular the problem of how people who are motivated by self-interest can cooperate, thereby allowing society to exist (a theme that Freud would turn to in the twentieth century). Because of the scarcity of resources in relation to the size of the population, people are forced to depend upon each other for subsistence. Smith agreed with Locke's assumption that all individuals would prefer to be self-sufficient, depending upon no other person, but the limited resources of the earth preclude such a situation. This view of the independent nature of man constitutes a critical difference between capitalist and socialist personality theory.

One product of man's self-interest is economic competition—individuals will produce the goods that satisfy men's wants at prices that will further their own interests. Similarly, purchasers, who are equally motivated by self-interest, will buy the goods offered at the best price. It is the competition from attempting to produce the best goods at the best price that keeps self-interest under control. Smith went on to show how this competition leads to the continuing improvement of society and the betterment of its members, and he emphasized that government tampering with the natural laws of the market weakens these laws to the detriment of all. Government interference in the marketplace amounts to subversion of man's most basic interests.

The Wealth of Nations is a book about economics, but within it are the assumptions about human nature that form the cornerstones for describing capitalist personality. First, Smith identified the basic motivation of life as being self-interest. This was an important step away from the religious belief that the purpose of life was to contemplate God or prepare for heaven.

Human beings are not by nature cooperative, they only cooperate because there are not enough resources for them to be self-sufficient. From this self-interest arises the epiphenomenon of competition. Men are naturally competitive, and they will only stop competing and cooperate with each other when it is in their own self-interest to do so. As Smith explained:

> Man has almost constant occasion for the help of his
> brethren, and it is in vain for him to expect it from

their benevolence only. He will be more likely to prevail
if he can interest their self-love in his favor, and show
them that it is for their own advantages to do for him
what he requires of them.

Implicit in The Wealth of Nations is the assumption that society
is oppressive to the individual. Whereas men are motivated to go out
and compete, society, and particularly government, often hampers
that natural competition. As men pursue their natural goals of pleasure,
they cannot avoid being in conflict with government, which will always
sacrifice the satisfactions of the people for the stability of the regime.
The interference of government into the lives of individuals, and particularly into their economic lives, is a travesty of human nature.
Even with those whom the government is supposed to be helping by
passing welfare or housing legislation are damaged by taking away
their basic motivation, the instinct to compete.

During the period 1975-80, Indochinese refugees living in California were eligible for special cash assistance programs for their
first three years in the United States. A family of two parents and two
children were eligible for $686, as well as food stamps and medicaid,
per month. This income was tax-free. Often these payments were
conditional on the refugee's being enrolled in English classes and
payment was forfeited if too many classes were missed.

Since many of the Indochinese refugees who came in the late
1970s were country people who had never had the opportunity to go to
school, they were often delighted to find that the U.S. government was
going to pay for their education. Furthermore, monthly support payments of $686 to an unskilled, non-English speaking father of two was
not much less than he could expect to earn on his own. The structure
of the system was such that, at least in the short run, it seemed to
reward those who stayed on welfare over those who took low-paying
jobs; not everyone who came from Vietnam had Mr. Nguyen's drive.
This is what Smith, and modern-day capitalist theorists such as Milton
Friedman, have in mind when they write about the pernicious effects
of removing incentives to compete. Not only is it harmful to the system, but it also leads to the erosion of character.

Parallel to their concern about the oppressive nature of government, capitalists also tend to reject any authority abiding outside the
individual. Given that men operate in their own self-interests, capitalist personality theory is hostile to any notion that an institution such
as the government or the church or society in general be allowed to
control man. The ultimate authority rests within the individual, not
in some outside order imposed upon him. The most virulent modern
spokesperson for this view that authority abides within is author Ayn
Rand.

Another capitalist assumption about human nature is that man is motivated by rational considerations. Seeking to better themselves, men will pursue those activities that bring them measurable gain. They are not, as a rule, motivated by religion, passions, or unconscious wishes. They look at the world through critical, discerning eyes, and attempt to transform that world in a logical and self-beneficial manner.

Finally, Adam Smith takes a melioristic view of human nature: society is constantly improving and will continue to do so as long as government does not act to subvert the natural competitive instincts of man. Again, economic practice reflects the natural desire of men for progress. Just as businessmen seek advantages over their competitors through improved methods of production, men are naturally inclined to work for the improvement of their own lives. Adam Smith stated that this desire for self-improvement "comes with us from the womb, and never leaves us till we go to the grave."

Given the materialistic bent of human nature, much improvement is likely to come through science and technology. Capitalists see the story of the human race as one of unfaltering progress, in which the technology brought about by economic competition has time and again proved to be man's salvation. As objectionable as some people find nuclear power plants today, they are part of the never-ending chain of human progress.

BENTHAM, SOMBART, AND HOLLAND

Another important influence in the rise of capitalist personality theory was the philosopher Jeremy Bentham. Bentham, who lived on the money his father had made in real estate speculations, is best known for his concept of utilitarianism. Utilitarianism holds that an act is right or good if it causes pleasure, bad if it leads to pain. Like the capitalist businessman, humans are motivated by the drives of maximizing profitability—i.e., pleasure—and minimizing their losses by avoiding pain. This is the basic idea behind modern sociological exchange theory.

In Bentham's view, social structure is the result of individuals recognizing that they must sacrifice some of their pleasures of the present for the greater good. The goal of the state is to allow men to achieve their particular pleasures. Bentham represents the extreme in rationalism: he introduced "Felicific Calculus" to help men determine the pain and pleasure inherent in any course of action. By use of this method, an individual is able to weigh the consequences of any act—going to work versus calling in sick, for example—and consider the pain and pleasure of all persons affected by the act. Utilitarianism aims for the greatest happiness for the greatest number of persons, based upon considerations of individual self-interest.

Werner Sombart (1863-1941), a German economist and sociologist and an influence on both Weber and Thorstein Veblen, is known for his attempt to describe psychological characteristics of capitalists. Although historian Arthur Mitzman has pointed out that Sombart's reputation was damaged irreparably by his flirtation with fascist ideology after World War I, Sombart was one of the most famous academicians of his time.

In The Quintessence of Capitalism (1915), Sombart suggested that there are two qualities necessary for the capitalist spirit in any individual: the "soul of the undertaker" (in the sense of entrepreneur rather than mortician), and the "soul of the respectable middle class."

Qualities in a successful capitalist personality, according to Sombart, include intelligence, especially in memory, cleverness in judging people and situations, imagination, an abundance of the "will to live," the need for achievement and ambition, and a lack of sensitivity.

Sombart also held that all European people held a "germ-capacity"—some sort of genetic tendency—for capitalism, and that it was particularly strong among two European groups. The "Heroic" peoples—the Romans, Normans, Lombards, Saxons, Franks, Venetians, Genoese, English, and Germans—furthered the development of trade through force, and the "Trading" peoples—the Florentines, Scotch, and Dutch—used standard commercial methods to develop trade. The Celtic peoples—the Highlanders, Irish, French, and Spanish—are no good at business, asserted Sombart, and what little ability the Spanish have comes from Jewish and Moorish influences.

With regard to the influence of religion on the development of capitalism, Sombart suggested that Catholicism, in addition to Protestantism, had all the qualities necessary to give rise to capitalism. The phenomenon of papal taxation in Italy necessitated the development of complex financial structures that paved the way for future trade. He particularly identified Aquinas as setting the stage for capitalism through his emphasis on becoming free of passion, the rationality of life, and the condemnation of all forms of cheating.

In The Jews and Modern Capitalism (1913), Sombart asserted that the rationalization of life is also found in Judaism, but that Judaism has never had an ideal of poverty such as is found in Catholic and Protestant works. As with Protestantism, Judaism has a theology that is congruent with capitalism. Sombart attributes Jewish success in business to the extreme nationalism of the Jews before nationalism developed in Christian countries, the lack of emphasis on the sanctity of poverty, and a different code of ethics for dealing with non-Jews than when dealing with Jews.

Sombart's theory, while interesting from a historical perspective, is basically a "race" theory that relies upon speculations about genetics for its basic hypotheses. As such, it stands at odds with the major point of this book, which is that personality and behavior are much more the products of social environment than they are products of "germ-capacities."

Although not an attempt to explain capitalism, modern-day psychologist John Holland's theory of vocational choice offers another explanation for the personality characteristics that are likely to be found with successful business enterprise. Holland's theory is based on the assumption that most people can be categorized within six personality types labeled Realistic, Investigative, Artistic, Social, Enterprising, or Conventional. With each type comes a set of personality characteristics widely distributed in the group. Although pure types are rare, the personalities of most people can be classified within two of the six categories. Most capitalists would be categorized as Enterprising types. Holland describes the so-called "E-type" personality as follows:

> The Enterprising type likes enterprising jobs such as salesperson, manager, business executive, television producer, sports promoter, buyer. Has leadership and speaking abilities but often lacks scientific ability.
> Is described as:
>
> | | | |
> |---|---|---|
> | Adventurous | Energetic | Self-confident |
> | Ambitious | Impulsive | Sociable |
> | Attention-getting | Optimistic | Popular |
> | Domineering | Pleasure-seeking | |

Holland also suggests that all environments can be classified as to the six types, and that the Enterprising type will seek enterprising environments. These enterprising environments, in turn, will reinforce the roles that allow him to demonstrate his personality characteristics. Individual differences in behavior are the result of the strength of the personality characteristics and the nature of the environment in allowing their expression. A Social type stuck in an Enterprising environment will be unable to express his social nature to the fullest; an Enterprising type in an Artistic environment will find his natural behavior hampered by the demands of the situation.

THE QUALITIES OF CAPITALIST MAN

Students of capitalist personality through the ages have identified a number of characteristics that seem to occur concurrently with successful capitalist enterprise. Whether these are the product of historical factors, religion, genetics, or environments, the capitalist personality can be identified by certain qualities that appear in its practitioners. As described by Reich in the previous chapter, the capitalist society, with its emphasis and values centered on commercialism, fosters these qualities and perpetuates their transmission to the next generation. Whereas certain individuals may manage to escape or avoid the influence of the pervasive capitalist culture (certainly many native-born Americans do not achieve Mr. Nguyen's success), the vast majority of people experience and are subject to its teachings throughout most aspects of their lives. Even in the most ostensibly value-free areas—academics, for example—success in a capitalist society is dependent upon marketing one's product, whether it be theories or can openers.

Capitalist theory starts with the view that freedom is natural and that the ultimate source of authority resides in man himself, rather than in a superimposed structure. Governments are necessary evils, subverting man's natural instincts, but they protect the individual and his property from the malevolence of others.

The basic motivation of man is his own self-interest. Satisfaction in life is most tangibly achieved by the acquisition of material goods. Certain personality characteristics or roles are necessary for this successful acquisition, including frugality, thrift, honesty, punctuality, dependability, ambition, optimism, achievement, and a certain kind of asceticism.

Man, in the capitalist framework, pursues his own self-interest in an essentially rational manner, optimizing his pleasure through the rational recognition of the costs and benefits of his actions. Through science and technology, man improves, and consequently society improves. Since the economic system is a reflection of the basic motivations and characteristics of man, its health and stability is an indication of the health and stability of a particular society. The imposition of authority where not needed leads to a kind of collective mental illness within some members of the society.

No one, not even Karl Marx, can dispute the achievements of the capitalist enterprise system. It has distributed material wealth among many segments of the population and made the accumulation of material goods available for all. Capitalist theorists suggest the failure of some individuals or groups to achieve material satisfaction comes from the interference of government or the lack of certain necessary personality traits within the individuals or groups themselves.

The achievements of capitalist technology aside, however, socialists argue that the capitalist theorists have inverted the explanation for the unhappiness of certain groups, and that this inversion is indicative of the basic fallacy of the capitalist view of human nature.

Socialist theorists further assert that this need to distort human nature as being centered on self-interest rather than human relations is endemic to Western social science which, naturally, reflects the values of capitalist society. In a famous series of researches at the Hawthorne plant of the Western Electric Company during the period 1927-39, for example, the Rockefeller Foundation funded a project in which Harvard psychologists studied the behavior of workers paid under a piece-rate system. Whereas new employees in this section tended to excel in production during the first days of their assignment, their performances eventually tapered off until they were in line with the much lower levels of the workers who had been on the line longer.

The Harvard psychologists explained this phenomenon of workers not performing in their own economic interests as being the result of confusion about payment under the piece-rate system. Critics who have taken a socialist perspective have pointed out that this condescending view of worker intelligence was an attempt to avoid recognizing the fundamental flaw of capitalist ideas about human nature: only in a system where human nature is perverted does self-interest become more important than the quality of human relations. The Western Electric workers chose to sacrifice material gain for harmonious relations within the work place.

Socialist personality theory, drawn from a long philosophical tradition of communitarianism and culminating in the works of Marx and Engels, is in agreement with capitalist theory in holding that life has the potential for constant improvement. But socialist theorists argue that in the United States and all capitalist societies, the system works to pervert the happiness of most of the people for the benefit of a few. Far from considering Mr. Nguyen's case an example of the rightness of the system, socialist theorists would relegate Mr. Nguyen's success to the perversion of his own personality and to the exploitation of others. Only through the coming of socialism will the full flowering of human nature and personal freedom in an industrial Garden of Eden be possible. In the socialist framework, Mr. Nguyen will not have to settle for mere monetary success.

4

Capitalist Character as the American Ideal

> Well, I'm not a scientist. I'm an inventor. Fara-
> day was a scientist. He didn't work for money.
> . . . Said he hadn't time to do so. But I do. I
> measure everything by the size of the silver dol-
> lar. If it don't come up to that standard then I
> know it's no good.
>
> Thomas Edison

As suggested earlier, Americans do not have a capitalist system because they value democracy and individual rights; rather they
value democracy and individual rights because they have a capitalist
system. Teachings of modern psychology to the contrary, the capitalist culture of the United States has undoubtedly been the major force
shaping the personalities of Americans. The force of this culture, as
we shall see, has both its good and bad effects. For in addition to
being surprised by the warmth and openness of Americans, foreigners
are often surprised at how crass, money-hungry, and opportunistic
Americans can be. A middle-aged, unmarried Vietnamese woman
once remarked to me that the available professional American men
she met seemed to be sizing her up as an investment first and as a
potential romantic partner second.

With the renewed interest in supply-side economics during the
1980s, Americans reaffirmed their belief in the teachings of Adam
Smith and the capitalist philosophers. But the influence of Adam Smith
has never been far removed from the American scene: from the time
of the Revolution through the fad of Social Darwinism, from Middletown to Milton Friedman, U.S. institutions have been shaping the personality characteristics that are necessary for capitalist enterprise.

Historian V. G. Wilhite has pointed out that delegates to the Constitutional Convention in 1787 were all professional men, over 50 percent of whom had loaned money to the new government to finance the revolution. Of the 55 delegates to the convention, 24 were professional money lenders, 11 were merchants and manufacturers, and 15 were slave owners. Holding firm to the ideas of Smith and Locke, the delegates sought to create a strong central government that would be protective of the economic order. Franklin and Hamilton, like most other delegates, were known to abhor the intervention of government in economic areas.

The extreme popularity of Social Darwinism in the United States is another phenomenon that grew out of the capitalist assumption that man is naturally a competitive, self-interested being. Darwinism as a personality theory and as an explanation for the success of the U.S. business system became extremely popular after the Civil War. Americans noted that Darwin's ideas about "survival of the fittest" and the "struggle for existence" seemed particularly appropriate metaphors for the practices of the business world. Economics, just as in the time of Calvin, was seen as an area for the development of character.

The most influential Social Darwinist (who happened to be British) was Herbert Spencer (1820-1903). Spencer believed that the problem of subsistence had a good effect on character because it led to only the fit surviving. Human beings, just as animals, were compelled to adapt to the environment in which they lived, and the state had no right to interfere in their lives. Spencer was against aid to the poor, who were by definition unfit, state-supported education, sanitation, housing regulations, or control of medical practice. He also opposed the establishment of public libraries on the grounds that it was wrong to give the people something for nothing and that libraries encouraged loafing.

With business as a reflection of the natural order, social changes that are counter to the interests of business are not only doomed to failure, but weaken the human race as a whole. During a speaking tour in 1882, Spencer suggested that the mixture of Aryan races in the United States would produce the finest species of humanity yet.

Human affairs, like those of nature, are subject to the laws of evolution, argued Social Darwinist William Graham Sumner of Yale, and men are foolish to think they can bring out change. In his essay, "The Absurd Effort to Make the World Over," Sumner wrote:

Everyone of us is a child of his age and cannot get out of it. He is in the stream and is swept along with it. All his sciences and philosophy come to him out of it. Therefore the tide will not be changed by us. It will swallow up both us and our experiments. . . . That is why it is the greatest folly of which a man can be capable, to sit down with a slate and pencil to plan out a new world.

MODERN CAPITALIST PERSONALITY

Modern economic theorists are no less circumspect than Adam Smith in drawing conclusions about human nature based upon economic principles. The notion that American business and American character are inseparable is a theme that pervades the writings of modern capitalist theorists such as Ayn Rand, Milton Friedman, and George Gilder. The implicit personality theory in Milton Friedman's works starts with the assumption that freedom is the ultimate goal of every human, but because men are "imperfect," social organization is necessary for social control. The basic problem of social organization is to coordinate market activities, and freedom must be reserved for responsible individuals only. The natural urge of men to compete must be perserved, and the freedom of American society is jeopardized whenever competition is hindered. On the issue of corporate social responsibility, Friedman writes:

> Few trends could so thoroughly undermine the very foundations of our free society as the acceptance by corporate officials of a social responsibility other than to make as much money for their stockholders as possible.

The capitalist view of human nature—the isolated individual seeking to create, enjoying liberty, and rejecting the chains of authority—continues virtually unmodified since the time of Adam Smith. The rise of supply-side economics ("Reaganomics") in the 1980s is simply a recycling of classical capitalist theory. George Gilder's paean to the supply side—Wealth and Poverty—blames the present disarray of the U.S. economy and disaffection within the social system on the government's subversion of the natural competitive instincts of man.

According to Gilder, the U.S. economy grew strong through the efforts of immigrants who expected no assistance from the government and who were allowed to pursue their goals unfettered. Through the establishment of welfare, social security, unemployment insurance, and other entitlements such as cash assistance programs for refugees, government has developed a system that dislocates natural structures and alienates people from themselves. Gilder's cure for the maladies of the U.S. economy is what Adam Smith would have recommended: Remove disincentives for work, cut government regulation of industry, and make the marketplace more competitive. These steps will bring the society and economy of the United States more in line with the natural order that is typical of capitalism and improve the mental and economic health of all Americans.

IDENTIFYING AMERICAN CHARACTER

After a comprehensive sampling of the literature prior to 1940, sociologist Lee Coleman published a list of what he saw as being qualities of the American character. These qualities included "associational activity, democracy and belief and faith in it, belief in the equality of all as a fact and as a right, freedom of the individual in ideal and in fact, disregard of law—direct action, local government, practicality, prosperity and general material well-being, puritanism, emphasis on religion and its great influence on national life, uniformity and conformity."

Unfortunately, Coleman's optimistic and somewhat simplistic list of "American traits" had been undermined some years earlier by Robert and Helen Lynd's study of American culture in the small Midwestern town of Muncie, Indiana in 1924. The Lynds had concluded that Americans were abandoning their belief in democracy for pecuniary culture: "the money medium of exchange and the cluster of activities associated with its acquisition drastically condition the other activities of the people." People had become obsessed with working, not for the sake of what satisfactions their work provided, but for money to acquire consumer goods.

> Thus this crucial activity of spending one's best energies year in and year out in doing things remote from the immediate concerns of living eventuates apparently in the ability to buy somewhat more than formerly, but both business men and working men seem to be running for dear life in this business of making the money they earn keep pace with the even more rapid growth of their subjective wants.

The Lynds found that citizens of Muncie were engaging in fewer public activities than previously and that they were in a process of redirecting their efforts toward consumerism rather than public service. Participatory democracy, which had been an important factor in 1890, had given way to the preoccupation with accumulating goods.

Although the Lynds felt that the culture of Muncie, Indiana was changing, more likely it was the culture of academic sociology that was changing. Social scientists were beginning to recognize that commercialism has always had a profound effect on American life and that this commercialism naturally effects the qualities that the culture rewards. Take, for example, the curious linkage between religion and business in the best-selling book of both 1925 and 1926, The Man Nobody Knows by Bruce Barton. The subject of The Man Nobody Knows was Christ, "the founder of modern business."

Barton, one of the founders of the modern advertising firm of Batten, Barton, Durstine and Osborn, wrote that Christ had been a tough and shrewd businessman who had been a successful carpenter, and who was so strong physically that no moneychanger in the temple had dared to challenge him. Additionally, he also "picked up twelve men from the bottom ranks of business and forged them into an organization that conquered the world."

The creation of the world was seen by Barton as a foreshadowing of the rise of twentieth-century advertising. The first four words ever uttered, "Let there be light," constitute the "charter" of advertising. "The brilliant plumage of the bird is color advertising directed to the emotions of its mate." Even the stars in the heavens were the "first and greatest electric sign."

Barton was not the only commentator of the period to link advertising and religion. Reverend Dr. S. Parkes Cadman, president of the Federal Council of Churches of Christ in America, wrote in a pamphlet distributed by the Metropolitan Casualty Insurance Company, "Moses was one of the greatest salesmen and real estate promoters that ever lived." Even President Coolidge recognized the religious nature of advertising. In a speech to the American Advertising Council, he stated that "advertising ministers to the spiritual side of trade." In another speech, Coolidge commented that "the man who builds a factory builds a temple, the man who works there, worships there." During the 1920s, Americans were confident that the plenitude of business opportunities was confirmation of both God's blessing and the "rightness" of the U.S. business system and its salutary affects on character.

A concern for the virtues necessary for the maintenance of the capitalist system are also apparent in anthropologist Margaret Mead's World War II study of American character. Mead stressed the American preoccupation with movement and success, as well as the invigorating effect of obstacles on Americans. In the words of Mead, Americans are "always moving, always readjusting, always hoping to buy a better car and a better radio." Historically, Americans have always lived in single families, isolated from kinship ties, so consequently the transmission of tradition to the younger generation tends to be a very faulty process. For this reason, child rearing tends to be left to institutions such as school or to the peer group. This lack of a past results in some distinct qualities in Americans: an emphasis on the individuality of each child, a concern for conformity, and a future orientation that stresses achievement. In Mead's view, love itself is a product of one's achievements in the U.S. capitalist culture: "We can recognize that yearning for achievement which is planted in every American child's breast by his mother's conditional smile." Reflecting the capitalist view that men are individualists with an infinite capacity for improvement, American culture teaches children that they cannot rely upon the accomplishments of others.

> Parenthood in America has become a very special thing,
> and parents see themselves not as giving their children
> final status and place, rooting them firmly for life in a
> dependable social structure, but merely training them
> for a race which they will run alone.

Anthropologist Francis L. K. Hsu has identified the American fear of dependence as the "core value" that pervades the culture. Whereas democracy and Christianity are the beliefs most highly touted, what Americans respect most is self-reliance. Hsu attributes this need for self-reliance to the general lack of security in American life (not surprising, considering the mother's conditional smile). This insecurity comes not only from the culture, where Americans are constantly moving and changing their lives, but from the family structure as well, where the rate of change has increased dramatically in recent years. Because Americans are so insecure, Hsu writes, they must rely upon personal success and achievement to give them a sense of identity.

In reviewing anthropological works on American culture, George and Louise Spindler recently noted the accelerated interest in applying techniques learned overseas to understanding cultural ideology at home. The Spindlers reported that among global works on American culture, ten qualities seemed to be recurrent: individualism, achievement orientation, equality, conformity, sociability, honesty, competence, optimism, work (positively valued), and authority (negatively valued). In a 30-year project focusing on the stability of these qualities, the Spindlers found that the most enduring of these aspects of American culture were equality, honesty, the value of work, independence, and sociability. Optimism about the future, tolerance of nonconformity, and the value of material success all exhibited much greater shifts in meaning and value to the participants in the Spindlers' study.

AMERICAN CHILD-REARING PRACTICES

The concept of achievement is found in virtually all studies of American character. Psychologist David McClelland has worked extensively with the concept of achievement motivation, which he defines as "competition with a standard of excellence." As children in any culture grow, McClelland suggests, they interact with a variety of stimuli. As they play with their toys, for example, either they learn to accept the toy as it is or they eventually become bored with it and look for something more complex and interesting.

If parents encourage the child's curiosity for more complex stimuli, then the child translates this interest into a need for achievement, which will generalize to the pursuit of success in academics, athletics, or other areas of life. Since business is the dominant feature of American culture, the child, as an adult, may translate his early achievement training into successful business enterprise. Need for achievement is not exclusively a capitalist phenomenon, however; McClelland found that children in noncapitalist cultures can have high levels of achievement motivation as well. Their culture would not direct this motivation toward business and commercialism, however.

But the role of the American parent in fostering need for achievement, or any other kind of need, may be changing. As any American over 40 who has children can testify, growing up in the United States is not like it used to be. Psychologist Urie Bronfenbrenner has commented:

> Particularly since World War II, many changes have occurred in patterns of child rearing in the United States, but their essence may be conveyed in a single sentence: Children used to be brought up by their parents.

In Bronfenbrenner's view, American society has changed so much that the process about which McClelland wrote may no longer prevail. Simply stated, American parents do not have enough time to raise their children anymore. As consumerism and inflation combined in the 1950s and 1960s to force mothers to work outside the home to provide additional income for their families, these families eventually became sufficiently dependent on the extra income so that the mothers could not quit working. By 1980, 50 percent of married American women and 80 percent of single women under 35 years of age were working. Of the women whose children are between the ages of 6 and 18, 60 percent are working. The prototypical television family of the 1960s—the Nelsons, the Cleavers, or the Stones—has virtually ceased to exist. According to Marvin Harris, the male-dominated, two-parent, multi-child breadwinner family now accounts for only 6 percent of the American population.

If American children are not being raised at home, then where are they being raised? Bronfenbrenner reports that the two institutions that have more or less taken on the job of socializing American children are the schools and television, which must be considered one of the ultimate institutions of consumerism in American life. Bronfenbrenner suggests that in modern America, children daily spend about equal amounts of time attending school and watching television. In comparison to children in the socialist culture of the Soviet Union, American children spend far less time talking, playing, or going out with adults. This is in spite of the fact that Soviet parents spend more time than American parents in working, commuting, and shopping. American parents are just too busy making money to raise their children.

PERPETUATING CAPITALISM

The obvious reason why socialists do so poorly in the U.S. electoral process is that most Americans cannot relate to socialist values. Coming from a tradition that stresses achievement, independence, commercialism, optimism, a belief in progress, and love being conditional upon achievement, then arguments about egalitarianism and worker solidarity are considerably less appealing than promises to make the economy blossom. As a rule, Americans are far more motivated by achievement and consumerism than by social relations, and it is naive to think that these values could ever change without a severe disruption of the American way of life. It is the nature of American culture to ensure that social values, as reflected in modern child-rearing practices, for instance, always remain subordinate to commercial values. Rosabeth Moss Kanter has pointed out, for example, that the pervasive practice of transferring American managers from state to state is less to widen their experience than to prevent them from forming attachments to neighbors and friends in the community rather than to the company.

American culture, founded upon the beliefs of John Locke and Adam Smith, attempts to perpetuate all the qualities that those philosophers found necessary for capitalist enterprise: an emphasis on freedom and personal responsibility, consumerism, self-interest, a distaste for government interference, and a belief in technological progress. The interest in the supply side in recent years is only a more radical demonstration of the most basic of American values.

Americans who sponsor refugees out of kindness are often naive about expecting their own cultural values to be found in all peoples. Americans of different ethnic heritages are sometimes unaware of how American culture has changed the values with which their grandparents arrived in the United States. It is not uncommon for a Polish-American family, for example, to sponsor a modern Polish refugee with the intention of helping that person much as someone had helped the American's grandfather decades ago—only to have the sponsorship turn out as a disappointment to all concerned. Neither the sponsor nor the refugee realizes how dependent he is upon a system of guaranteed jobs, free medical care, education, and housing. The refugee from the socialist society fails to find a place to live, fails to find a job, and seems satisfied to have acquired a pair of designer jeans and a Walkman. He doesn't seem to care about the kind of self-reliance that the American family keeps urging him to pursue. Worse yet, he doesn't even seem to mind his dependent status. Socialist culture has not taught him the roles that capitalist society rewards nor the need to strive for the things that Americans find important. The Polish refugee has been taught a set of roles for life in a society with a vastly different set of values.

5

Socialism and the Restoration of Human Character

> The own individual will of the servant, more closely regarded, is canceled in the fear of the master, and reduced to the internal feelings of its negativity. . . . This renunciation of individuality as self is the moment [phase] through which self-consciousness makes the transition to the universal will, the transition to positive freedom.
>
> Hegel

Just as modern Western personality theories are often said to be merely answers to Freud, socialist personality theory begins with an answer to Smith and his capitalist fellow travelers. Marx's goal, like that of Smith, was more to dissect and describe the workings of the economic system of his day than to write a theory of personality. As with capitalist theory, however, Marxist theories are built upon a foundation of ideas about human nature that gives socialism an implicit theory of personality.

Like capitalism, socialism is also a theory of optimism, but it is a theory of injustice as well—an explanation of how, throughout history, the greediness of a few has denied the true expression of human nature for everyone else. Far from being an accurate reflection of human character, capitalism has sacrificed man's humanness so that a few can acquire wealth. In the capitalist system, the people on the bottom are condemned to live their lives in misery because modern capitalists, like Calvin or Herbert Spencer before them, are convinced that there is something wrong with people who don't succeed in the capitalist system. Socialists share the suspicions of capitalists about government, but they hold that the danger of most government is that it serves the interests of the wealthy rather than those of the ordinary person.

Marx began to write at a time when the huge discrepancy between Smith's rosy description of the ameliorizing qualities of capitalism and the actual facts of what it was like to work in a nineteenth-century factory was becoming increasingly apparent. Even at the time Smith was writing, a large segment of the British population lived in the most desperate poverty. Marvin Harris has suggested that, for the British working classes, life at the time of Marx was as miserable as it had been 500 years before during the Black Death.

> Certain facts seem incontrovertible. The larger machines
> became, the longer and harder the people who ran them
> had to work. By the 1800's, factory hands and miners
> were putting in twelve hours a day. . . . At day's end,
> after contending with the continuous whine and chatter of
> wheels, shafts, dust, smoke, and foul odors, the opera-
> tors of the new labor-saving devices retired to their dingy
> hovels full of fleas and lice. As before, only the wealthy
> could afford meat. Rickets, a new crippling disease of
> the bones caused by a lack of sunshine and dietary sources
> of vitamin D, became endemic in the cities and factory
> districts. The incidence of tuberculosis and other dis-
> eases typical of low-grade diet also increased.

In 1770, just six years before the publication of The Wealth of Nations, over half the people born in Europe died before they were 15 years old. Harris alleges that the 540 percent increase in crime in England between 1805 and 1833 is attributable to the increasing desperation of the working class. Where was the inevitable improvement in society that Smith had predicted capitalism would deliver?

The beginnings of socialist personality theory are traceable not to a critique of capitalist philosophy, but rather to Hegel's (1770–1831) ideas on the nature of society. Hegel had argued that one of the fundamental principles of life was that everything leads to its opposite: that the conditions and ideas of the world that are contradictory always unite to create something higher and more complex. This dialectical process was the basis for Marx's interpretations of the influence of economics upon personality.

At Berlin University where he studied in 1835–41, Marx was a member of the Doctor's Club, an informal student group organized around the study of Hegel. This group, which was inspired and excited by the philosopher's works, was known as the Young Hegelians.

In 1841, Ludwig Feuerbach, himself a Young Hegelian, published his analysis of Hegel's works in The Essence of Christianity. In this book, Feuerbach argued that Hegel had made a mistaken assumption about the nature of the real world. It is not the divine that is the "real." Rather, God is a fantasy onto which man has projected his own powers. The stronger man believes God to be, the weaker he considers his own powers. The purpose of creating a God, Feuerbach believed, is to provide an ideal to which man can compare himself. The purpose of religion is to create a world in which man can strive to be better and bring peace and harmony to all. In other words, God did not create man to serve his own purposes, man created God to serve man's purposes.

In the Theses on Feuerbach (1845), Marx attacked Feuerbach for not going far enough in his thinking about man and religion. Whereas Feuerbach's proposition that man creates God and not vice versa was earth-shaking in the context of nineteenth-century university life ("Enthusiasm was general: we all became at once 'Feuerbachians,'" wrote Engels), Marx felt that Feuerbach had failed to recognize the truly revolutionary point: that the importance of the nonreligious aspects of society—the activities of everyday life in which people spend most of their time—is far greater than life's religious aspects.

However important one may believe one's religion to be, it almost always constitutes a very small place in the actual day-to-day lives of most people. For the majority of people secular forces—such as earning a living and supporting a family—are far more powerful than any ideas about God. Belief in God, in fact, is a luxury which comes after basic physiological needs are met (an idea later to be popular in Western humanistic psychology), or it is a means for denying the wretchedness of one's conditions. However insightful Feuerbach had been, he had missed the real point by ignoring importance in the practical world of "human sensuous activity"—the material world in which we all live. Marx argued that the serious activity of philosophy must concern itself with the here and now, and not the utopianism of how we might use religion to bring harmony to all.

Herein we have the cornerstone of implicit Marxist personality theory: when we make assumptions about the world and the people in it we have to start from the material world and not the divine or even ideological world. We cannot invoke mystical concepts such as Calvin's predestination or Freud's "anatomy is destiny" to explain events that occur in the real world. We can only theorize about those phenomena that we know exist.

The materialist basis of Marxist theory does not mean, of course, that Marx believed economics was the sole important consideration in life. The materialist aspect of Marxist theory simply means that, when explaining any phenomenon, we have to deal with what can be observed and deduced given life as it is lived in the world. It is important to note that, in spite of its emphasis on rational thought, the capitalist system is much less strict on this point. The capitalist system has been able to take nonmaterialist concepts such as God and survival of the fittest and use them in the service of the market. The necessity of starting from a materialist outlook might be called the first law of Marxist personality theory.

The second cornerstone of Marxist personality theory concerns the nature of consciousness, the way in which people interpret information about the world that is transmitted through their senses. This was a topic that Marx and Engels dealt with extensively in The German Ideology (1845-46). During the nineteenth and early twentieth century, people widely subscribed to a theory of human development called "recapitulation." The spokesperson for this view in American psychology was G. Stanley Hall, who is associated with the theory that "Ontogeny recapitulates phylogeny."

Recapitulation theory holds that the mental development of every child reflects the development of human thought from savagery to civilization. Marx and Engels, on the other hand, argued that consciousness, like language, evolved from man's need to interact with other men, and because the relations between men change through history, so does the nature of their consciousness. What men think is a product of the human world around them—their relations with other men—and not some kind of immanent categories of cognitive development stretching back to prehistory. People don't evolve through stages of thinking as savages as babies, the barely civilized as teenagers, and analytic philosophers as adults.

Men share many qualities with animals, but the nature of man's consciousness is one of the areas that sets him apart. In contrast to capitalist theory, which holds that the nature of consciousness does not change through society's uninterrupted march of progress, Marx held that what we think is a product of the conditions around us. Consciousness is a product of social forces in the environment.

But the most important premise in Marxist personality theory is that the essence of man is what Marx called "the ensemble of social relations." This fundamental belief is introduced in the Theses on Feuerbach and is constantly referred to throughout later socialist literature. The socialist belief in man's social, rather than self-interested, nature is counter to the beliefs of the capitalist philosophers from Hobbes to Friedman and is probably the most important factor differentiating socialist personality theory from capitalist. Whereas most Western psychologists have tended to regard man as a kind of rugged individualist whose essence lay in some mystical and certainly not material "self" within the body, socialist theorists have totally rejected this notion. In their view, man does not exist outside social relations. Personality is formed through interaction with others, and if there is no interaction, there can be no personality.

The view of the capitalist philosophers that runs through most Western psychological theory holds that men must give up some of their essential nature in order to have society. In so doing, they deny a basic part of their individualities, but it is a sacrifice necessary for civilization. In a collective of any kind, men lose some of their identities.

In Marxist terms, this notion that men lose their personalities when they join together in society is ridiculous—only by having society can men have individual personalities at all. Without society, men would be bundles of instincts like the animals—like sheep, to use Marx's example—totally alike with no distinguishing characteristics. The most basic motivation in life is to have rewarding social relations. Men do not desire to be alone or to work for their prosperity only. Nor do they resent controlling some of their impulses for the sake of society. Only the perverted personality enjoys selfish activity that may bring harm or deprivation to others or cares only about his own enrichment. The social life of man and his relationships to others is the most basic element of study in trying to understand human personality. Hypothesizing about motivations and characteristics of men outside the context of their social relations, as the capitalist philosophers have done, is a worthless enterprise bound to lead to an illusional view of human nature.

In constructing their theories about the nature of man, the capitalist philosophers have made what modern social scientists would call a sampling error. They derived their notions about what people are like by looking only at those who were successful in the capitalist system. (In contrast to Marx, Smith, Bentham, and Locke were all quite comfortable financially by the end of their lives.) As Marx commented on Bentham:

> With the driest naivete he assumes that the modern petty bourgeois, especially the English petty bourgeois, is the normal man. Whatever is useful to this peculiar kind of normal man, and to his world, is useful in and for itself. He applies this yardstick to the past, the present and the future.

The capitalist philosophers, in Marx's opinion, have simply created a world based upon their prejudices about what the world should be. When writing about capitalism as an extension of human nature, they have ignored the fact that the great mass of people do not seem to be benefiting from this so-called natural order. The philosophers have failed to look at the world as it really is, interpreting the increased wealth of a few as evidence for the fact that life will always get better and that preoccupation with the acquisition of capital is the natural state of human affairs. They have considered only their own experiences and misinterpreted human nature.

THE SOCIALIST PREHISTORY OF MAN

At no time in history, write Marx and Engels, did individuals exist as solitary hunters. Like apes, men were born into groups, and the notion of solitary men making it on their own à la Robinson Crusoe is a capitalist invention, possible only in a highly developed technological society. In the beginning of history, men lived together and shared the resources—including the women. In the beginning, the need to cooperate in order to survive in a hostile world necessitated mutual toleration between group members. During this period came the flowering of human nature. Men did not compete, but rather were able to focus on developing their abilities and on the quality of human relations.

Although it is difficult to imagine caveman times as being the idyll of human civilization, life in the days of prehistory may not have been so desperate as once thought. Marvin Harris suggests that the diet of the caveman was far superior to our diets today, and that men had to spend only about three hours daily in pursuit of food, and women three hours in preparing it. The rest of the time was spent in leisure and creative activities. This prehistoric division of labor was again attributable to relative physical strength. However, as life became less hostile and population became more dense, competition for women and other resources began to arise. As human emotion and individuality became more pronounced, rules for conduct in the group became necessary for the maintenance of harmony. Promiscuity gave way to group marriage, which in turn gave way to the "pairing family."

The pairing family had as its base the relationship between one man and one woman, although polygamy and occasional infidelity was allowed for the man but not for the woman. These relationships were easily dissolved and in most cases the children remained with the mother. Because the males were more likely to leave the family, women generally had supremacy in the society because they had greater influence over the next generation.

Due to economic factors, however, the family eventually began to stabilize. The larger the family, the more opportunities to gain wealth through animals and herding. As wealth became more and more identified with family groups rather than with the tribal groups, males tended to leave the family less often. Increased productivity necessitated workers from outside the family, and hence the beginnings of slavery. The rise of the "monogamian society" was the beginning of civilization as we know it today. Its aim was to have children of undisputed paternity who would inherit the wealth of the family. The males who were attracted to the increasing wealth of the family overthrew the matriarchy, and women's work became restricted to the home and the children. According to Engels, the overthrow of the matriarchy was the beginning of class warfare:

> The first class antagonism which appears in history coincides with the development of the antagonism between man and woman in monogamian marriage, and the first class oppression, with that of the female sex by the male. Monogamy was a great historical advance, but at the same time it inaugurated, along with slavery and private wealth, that epoch, lasting until today, in which every advance is likewise a relative regression, in which the well-being and development of one group are attained at the repression and misery of the other.

As the division of labor took root in the family, it began to take root in society as well. People were no longer generalists, able to fill all their own needs and living in harmony. They took on specific activities and began to define themselves as categories: "hunter," "fighter," "shaman," "food preparer," etc. Opportunity for accumulating wealth was dependent on status, and the heads of tribes became increasingly wealthy. In the feudal period, the wealthy began to need workers from outside the family to do the work that the slaves could not do. The poor placed themselves under the protection of the powerful by working their land. Property became more and more important, and consequently women's role within the household became less important.

Engels says that at this point occurred the second great division of labor—the separation of handicrafts manufactured in the home from agricultural labor, leading to the phenomenon of the "expert," the person specializing in a specific kind of task. The family, and particularly the work of the male outside the family, became the economic unit of society. Increasing population required more rules to manage society and protect the property of the wealthy, so governments became more and more powerful. Disproportion in the accumulation of wealth began to make wars necessary for its redistribution.

As the size of the family grew, there was less and less land for everyone. People began to move to the towns in search of work. At this critical moment of human history, Engels notes, we see the beginning of the phenomenon of the "middleman," the capitalist exploiter:

> Here a class appears for the first time which, without taking any part in production, captures the management of production as a whole and economically subjugates the

producers to its rule; a class that makes itself the indispensable intermediary between two producers and exploits them both.

The subjugation of the working class was the culmination of a historical process that changed men's consciousness and denigrated all human relations. The natural ethic of human cooperation dating from tribal days ended as men turned into commodities who sold their labor and hence themselves to the highest bidder. The struggle for existence in a world that had come to be dominated by factories, time schedules, and dehumanizing divisions of labor destroyed the feelings of sharing and brotherhood men had known in the beginning of history. Even Adam Smith recognized the high cost of the necessity of selling oneself to a factory owner and its deadening effect on human faculties:

> The man who works upon brass and iron, works with instruments and upon materials of which the temper is always the same, or very nearly the same. But the man who plows the ground with a team of horses or oxen, works with instruments of which the health, strength, and temper, are very different upon different occasions. . . . His understanding, however being accustomed to a greater variety of objects, is generally much superior to that of the other, whose whole attention from morning till night is occupied in performing one or two very simple operations. How much the lower ranks of people in the country are really superior to those of the town, is well known to every man whom either business or curiosity has led to converse much with both.

The men of Marx's day were no longer in touch with their true human essence or "species-being," no more so than the members of present-day capitalist societies. Economic considerations necessitated the sacrifice of the true nature of man in order to survive in a world increasingly dominated by overpopulation and the accumulation of capital.

SOCIALIST PERSONALITY THEORY

According to Marxist theory, we cannot look at people in the West today and see a natural human personality. Any person who is a product of a system where the accumulation of capital and the emphasis on having and consuming is paramount has a warped personality. To use a Marxist term, people today suffer from alienation, a feeling of estrangement from themselves and the world around them. They have lost the qualities that make them human.

As suggested earlier, the capitalist model of personality holds that the pursuit of profit as a reflection of man's basic self-interest is the prime motivator of people. Rather than being an extension of human nature, the philosopher Marek Fritzhand has argued that Marx believed that the pursuit of profit is a burden that is unnatural to man. Life is meaningful, according to Marx, only when man lives intensely and thoroughly, when he has the opportunity to realize all his abilities and doesn't have to worry about satisfying his material needs.

Man is not naturally self-seeking. Man is by nature creative, seeking beauty, truth, and good. Through positive service to other men, and hence to society, man finds satisfaction at the same time that he finds his individuality. He knows no conflict between economic and moral values, and there is no distinction between his personal and societal lives. Aggression and violence are only the products of the pursuit of material goods and not intrinsic to human nature. Man is grateful for the opportunity to control some of his impulses for the benefit of others.

The pursuit of capital has led to a perversion of human nature. While a very small minority of individuals live well—and they are not free either, says Engels, since they sacrifice their humanity and become slaves to their capital—the vast majority of people continue to suffer because they must live with economic deprivation and alienation from their true species-being. According to Marx, the first step in rectifying this situation is through a redistribution of wealth.

How can the redistribution of wealth return to man the essence of his personality that was lost centuries ago with the rise of capitalism? Marx argues that through his labor, man transforms the environment, which in turn acts to transform man himself. Personality is therefore a process that changes as the environment changes. Man can change in accordance with his relationships to the environment and to other men. Because of the importance of work and its effects on every part of life, working conditions are the greatest single influence on personality. Changing those conditions will bring about the quickest and most complete change in human personality.

Another way to improve the lives of men is to remove the class structure so that all can benefit from economic prosperity. Social scientists have long been aware that social class has a critical effect on health, for example, with people of the lower classes more likely to suffer from arthritis, hypertension, neuralgia, and tuberculosis, while people of the upper class suffer from hives, colitis, and hay fever. Along the same lines, constipation is a disease of the lower classes, diarrhea of the upper. Schizophrenia is found among members of the bottom of society, neurosis among the top. Psychologist Robert Hogan lists the following areas of social behavior that can be predicted from social class: quality and style of dress, personal hygiene, posture and physical mannerisms, speech habits, intellectual style, type and location of house within one's community, education level, annual income, child-rearing practices, religious preferences, political beliefs, and style and frequency of sexual intercourse. Social class even relates to waist size, with lower-class people tending to be heavier. Social class, in other words, limits one's individuality and subverts individual development.

These opinions about the lost nature of individuals and the events that led to that loss allow us to derive some postulates that summarize Marxist personality theory. First, Marx would hold that when a child is born, he or she probably has within the seeds of creativity, cooperation, and love for humanity. Since personality is a process, however, and not something given genetically or through a "self" within, the child's natural endowments will be shaped by factors in the environment. Unfortunately, the child is at the mercy of the warped personalities of its parents, as well as the emotional and economic deprivations characteristic of the capitalist environment.

The mother, in Marx's time, (and in sharp contrast to either the United States or the Soviet Union today) stays at home taking care of the family's domestic needs while the father is outside trying to meet the family's economic needs. Although both of them also once carried seeds of creativity, these have been sacrificed so that the family unit can compete more effectively in the marketplace. Most children will know economic shortages, but more importantly, they will also know a shortage in the natural warmth and love of their parents.

Given these inherent shortages in the home into which a child is born, the seeds of creativity cannot survive. The child grows up emotionally crippled, never knowing the potential that lies within him and never knowing truly satisfactory human relations. One lesson that he does learn, however, is to compete: the persons who get ahead—that is, those who know less economic deprivation—are those who are able somehow to outdo the people around them. The child quickly learns that life is a race that goes not to the swift, but to the economically advantaged. Because of this competition, truly meaningful social relationships are never allowed to flourish. And without meaningful social relationships, man is barely human.

The educational system reinforces this situation by socializing people to accept at face value the lives that lay before them, and it further reinforces the sexual division of labor, encouraging men to make work, and not their families or relationships with other men, the primary motivation in their lives. Similarly, according to Engels, women are forced to make home, husband, or children their primary motivations. The importance of religion in this scenario is not, as

Feuerbach suggested, that it gives humans an ideal to live up to so that life can be made better for all. Rather, religion distracts people from the misery, injustice, and truly antihuman qualities of the lives they are forced to live.

To summarize Marxist personality theory, we can say that men are products of their environments, and specifically the economic environments in which they live; the essence of human life is in social relations, not in the pursuit of self-interest; human nature has been perverted with the rise of capitalism and it will be returned to its pristine state with the establishment of communism; and man is naturally a seeker of truth, good, beauty, and that he has unlimited potential for self improvement.

Socialist theory is congruent with capitalist theory in the belief that man is essentially a rational being and that governments are oppressive. The reason for the oppressive nature of government differs between theories, however. Whereas the capitalists believe that governments subvert the basic instincts of man and suppress his real self-expression, socialists argue that governments are agents of the class that is on top.

In a socialist framework, men do not move from individuality and agree to form society, but only through society do men develop individual personalities. The only reason men are so thoroughly self-interested is because they are products of the warped values of capitalist economics. Freed of the pressures of that system, men will return to valuing human relationships. The basic human instinct in implicit socialist personality theory is the desire for rewarding human relationships.

Lenin, Trotsky, Stalin, and ostensibly all the members of the 1917 vanguard subscribed to these assumptions about human nature. Lenin set forth the task of making a "New Soviet Man"—a full flowering of human nature designed to fit the new economic, political, and social order being established in the Soviet Union. Through revolutionary activity, Lenin said, the new man was going to recapture all that had been sacrificed in the rise of capitalism.

At the same time in history that Lenin was directing social scientists to begin creating the New Soviet Man, John B. Watson of the United States was promising a new world order based upon the principles of behaviorism, and Freud was arguing that human nature precluded any improvement of life on earth whatsoever. Early in the twentieth century, psychology began taking over from philosophy the task of identifying the qualities that constitute human nature.

As Marx would have predicted, however, a close scrutiny of the psychological theories of personality in both the United States and the Soviet Union reveal that, like all ideas, they are more products of the consciousnesses of their proponents than they are scientific approaches to understanding human nature.

6

Id, Ego, and Economic Theory

[Freud] discovered all the filth of which human
nature is capable—and it is notorious that it would
require a lifetime to make even a rough inventory
of it. . . . The end-product of the Freudian method of explanation is a detailed elaboration of man's
shadow-side such as had never been carried out
before. It is the most effective antidote imaginable
to all idealistic illusions about the nature of man.

Jung

When Thomas Carlyle read Malthus's views on population in
1798 and labeled economics "the dismal science," he could not have
foreseen the American fascination with psychoanalysis, the truly dismal science of the twentieth century. Freud's initial optimism about
understanding human nature through an understanding of childhood sexual instincts eventually gave way to a world view far more pessimistic
than Malthus had conceived. Whereas Malthus had argued that we are
all bound to unhappiness because spiraling populations overwhelm
available resources, Freud concluded that we would be unhappy if we
were the only people on earth. As depressing as the laws of supply and
demand may be, they don't compare with the intrapsychic misery that
comes from the unfulfilled wishes of childhood, the struggle with one's
parents, and the terrible price mankind pays for civilization.

According to psychoanalytic theory, human nature is the same
in the United States, the Soviet Union, or Timbuktu. Americans, Soviets, Cubans, Cambodians, and all human beings are motivated by
the same sexual and aggressive drives, and though these drives may
take different forms of expression in different cultures people are all

47

basically alike. In all societies these drives have to be controlled in order for civilization to continue to exist. But Freud's view of civilization has little in common with the civilizations of Adam Smith or Karl Marx. In Freud's view, all societies are products of the collective neuroses of their members. In contrast to the melioristic views of both capitalist and socialist theories, psychoanalysis sees no hope for improvement of the human condition except through the control of the most basic human drives. All religions, philosophies, and economic policies are little more than means men use to deceive themselves about what they really want. The origin of human misery is not, as Karl Marx believed, an oppressive economic system. Rather human misery has its origin in the psychologically violent and sexually charged atmosphere of the family.

With behaviorism, psychoanalysis has been—and continues to be—one of the most influential approaches to understanding human nature in the West. For reasons to be discussed later, the psychoanalytic approach does not fit well with socialist ideology and consequently has been discouraged in the Soviet Union. But in the West, untold thousands of individuals have experienced psychoanalytically oriented psychotherapy in order to understand their id motivations, to resolve unfinished Oedipal conflicts, and to learn to strengthen their ego assets. Psychoanalysts and psychoanalytic psychotherapists have helped people to understand their instincts and to adjust to the misery and psychic violence that all of us experienced in the earliest years of life.

THE SEXUAL INSTINCT

Through the early years of his practice, Freud found what he considered overwhelming evidence that the sexual drive is the most basic force in human nature and that adult sexual relationships are reflective of the early sexual relationships within one's family. Every client who came to his couch seemed to be fixated upon problems relating to sexual feelings or activity. Worse yet, the sexuality that caused the real problems was not shenanigans of the adult years, but feelings and wishes dating from earliest childhood, usually directed toward one's parents. In the famous case of Dora, for example, the cause of her hysterical cough and hoarseness as an adult was traced back through a tangled maze of sexually tinged memories that eventually related her father's affair with a friend of the family to a watery discharge from a vaginal infection as a child. The theme of sexuality ran like a thread through the most mundane events in the lives of all the people Freud saw.

Freud came to believe that infants are born with powerful sexual instincts that begin to manifest immediately after birth. The focus of the erogenous life of children changes as they mature, centering on first the mouth, then the anus, and finally, the phallus, or where the phallus would be in the case of little girls. During the phallic period, little boys and girls evidence an almost uncontrollable attraction to the parent of the opposite sex. At the same time, they reject the parent of the same sex, competing with him or her in a none too subtle manner for the attention of the beloved.

For little boys, this attraction ends when the child recognizes the physical strength of his father and the potential violence inherent in continued competition. Little girls, in contrast, do not come to such a recognition of the strength of their mothers, and consequently emerge from the Oedipal/Electra period with much weaker superegos. This recognition of the dangers of continued competition with the parent of the same sex and the consequent repression of sexual feelings toward the parent of the opposite sex is a critical factor in normal child development. Rather than being an experience of psychopathology, Freud felt the Oedipal period occurred in all children in all cultures and was necessary for psychological maturity.

As the years pass, Freud believed, the dark and powerful wish for sexual union with our parents becomes increasingly masked by symbols so as to allay the anxiety of recognizing how we really felt as children. These symbols are most obvious in dreams, but in actual fact they intrude into every part of our lives: in jokes, religious practices, and art; in choice of occupation and mate, and in personal habits and tastes. It is this thwarted desire for sexual union with one of our parents that makes all of us, regardless of social class or economic situation, basically neurotic and unhappy. For while the wishes of the child can never be fulfilled, those wishes remain just below the surface throughout his or her life. As we try to sublimate—i.e., find substitutions for what we really want—we run from our basic motivations. Since sublimation is never as good as the desired object, we are all doomed never to be satisfied.

Freud felt that the Oedipal and Electra conflicts appeared in all families in all cultures and that their appearance in children during the ages of three to five is necessary for normal psychological development. Since the family structure in socialist society is just as likely to deny the sexuality of children as the family structure in capitalist society, socialist adults are just as likely to be unhappy as capitalist adults. In the orthodox Freudian viewpoint, normal adjustment in any society requires a resolution or acceptance of feelings from the Oedipal or Electra conflicts.

THE RISE OF PSYCHOANALYTIC CIVILIZATION

Unlike the civilization myths of Harris and Engels, the Freudian myth about the origin of society postulates no easy living or harmonious relations at the beginnings of history. In the Freudian view, civilization is an unhappy compromise that is the symbolic expression of how we feel about our fathers.

In the beginnings of history, Freud wrote in Totem and Taboo (1913), mankind lived together in a primal horde. The primal horde was dominated by a cruel father, stronger and more forceful than any of the other members of the tribe. The primal father kept all the resources, including the women, for himself, and he forced the young males to live on the outskirts of the tribe. Sons who fell out of favor with the father were castrated, killed, or driven off.

Eventually, however, the sons came to realize their collective strength. They united and killed the father, ate his body, and went on a rampage of orgy and incest. As the sun rose the next day, however, the sons were overcome with tremendous feelings of guilt for what they had done. Their society was destroyed, no one was strong enough to take the place of the father, and the group had no leader to ensure their survival. At this point in prehistory, the sons began to make the convenants necessary to protect society that Hobbes had also hypothesized. The purpose of these agreements was to make certain that the natural instincts of men would never again be expressed in such a destructive and wanton manner.

The young men agreed to restrict sexual activity and to abide by a complex set of rules that primitive peoples call taboos. They agreed to follow and obey a symbolic leader who would not necessarily be the strongest. The primal father became a god to whom they prayed for forgiveness of their sins. In the morning after the primal murder, civilization was born. Economics and other phenomena of civilization came much later and are merely symbolic expressions of the instincts that ran wild that fateful night.

Robert Hogan has suggested a number of important implications that derive from Freud's theory of the rise of civilization. First, history is a series of rebellions against authority that are traceable to instinctual factors. Residue from that night live within all of us and is acted out in the Oedipal and Electra phases of development. In order for children to be "civilized" to the rules of society, this drama must be reenacted on the small battlefield of intrafamilial rivalry. Just as the little boy competes with his father for mommy's attention, so will that competition manifest itself in any situation where men have authority over others.

Second, society is indeed a social contract, where men have agreed on rules simply to have order and avoid anarchy. Rather than being an economic unit, the purpose of the family is to teach the rules of the contract. In Freud's view, however, these destructive drives are not far below the surface in even the most civilized individuals:

> Men are not gentle creatures who want to be loved and who at the most can defend themselves if they are attacked; they are, on the contrary, creatures among whose instinctual endowments is to be reckoned a powerful share of aggressiveness. As a result, their neighbor is for them not only a potential helper or sexual object, but also someone who tempts them to satisfy their aggressiveness on him, to exploit his capacity for work without compensation, to use him sexually without his consent, to seize his possessions, to humiliate him, to cause him pain, to torture and kill him.

Third, belief in the beneficence of any ruler or authority figure is naive. Rebellion against authority is a product of human history, and children need to experience this rebellion in order to reach psychological maturity.

Finally, all history can be seen as a symbolic attempt to reinstate the primal father. No matter how repressive a regime, the people will eventually replace their ruler with someone equally tyrannical. Events such as the fall of the regime of the shah and his replacement by the Ayatollah Khomeini, the replacement of the monarchy of Cambodia with the Khmer Rouge, or that of the feudal system of Ethiopia with a totalitarian socialist regime are evidence that human instincts preclude progress. In the Freudian system, progress is a chance occurrence of history.

AMERICAN PSYCHOANALYTIC FAMILY LIFE

The Freudian version of the origins of civilization has been criticized on a number of grounds, particularly by anthropologists who argue that a tribe composed of members so antagonistic toward each other could not have survived in prehistoric times. Freud's story of the Oedipal and Electra conflicts, on the other hand, have not been so easily dismissed. Many anthropologists, in fact, have agreed with Freud that the Oedipal and Electra conflicts are universal, found in both primitive and modern societies. These theorists accept the psychoanalytic notion that rebellion against the father or authority figure seems to be a necessary part of psychological development irrespective of culture.

If, as the psychoanalysts argue, rebellion against a father figure is necessary for the healthy development of children, demographic trends in American families suggest that the next generation is going to have some trouble maintaining civilization as we know it now. As suggested earlier, the large-scale entry of women into the work force has brought dramatic changes in American family structure. According to the psychoanalytic viewpoint, these are changes that can only have a deleterious effect on American society.

Earlier I suggested that the prototypical family of working father/ child-raising mother has become a vanishing species, having given way to more and more dual earner and single parent households. In 1978, in fact, 51 percent of American families had both father and mother working an average of 42.6 hours per week in nonmanagerial jobs. According to sociologists George Masnick and Mary Jo Bane, the number of dual earner families will increase an additional 30 percent by 1990. Although these families will have more money to buy consumer goods, they will also have less time for interaction between family members.

More significant from a psychoanalytic view, however, is the startling rise in the number of households headed by women. By the end of the 1970s, 14 percent of American families were headed by divorced, separated, widowed, or never-married women, and 17 percent of all the children in the United States were living in families headed by a woman. This trend toward female-headed families reflects the growing number of divorces in the United States: in 1979, there was one divorce for every two marriages. In spite of the fact that 75 percent of all divorced people remarry, 45 percent of these second marriages end in divorce. And, of course, it is widely believed in American society that divorce has a negative effect on the psychological development of children.

Economists Sar A. Levitan and Richard S. Belous suggest, however, that the real damage to children in these families is economic. Since American working women earn only about 60 percent of what men earn, single parent families have less time to spend with and less money to spend on children. Although they tend to spend the same amounts on housing as married parents, and in spite of the fact that 70 percent of single parents work, considerably less money is available for food, clothing, and recreation. The biggest expense for single parents tends to be childcare, which takes up a significant part of the budget when salaries are low. In 1978, in fact, only 21.7 percent of working women held professional or management jobs, with the rest working in the relatively low-paying areas of clerical, service sales, or other nonprofessional types of employment. Although the number of women in management positions increased 80 percent between 1970 and 1980 (compared to a 12 percent increase for males), women still constitute only 5 percent of all management positions, and less than 1 percent of the very highest positions.

Irrespective of economics, however, is the psychological effect of being raised in a family where the parents are always working or absent. According to the psychoanalytic view, the outlook for these children is not good. Because these children are unlikely to experience a successful resolution of the Oedipal or Electra complexes, they are going to experience severe disruption in their psychological development. Young boys whose fathers are no longer present may see themselves as what psychoanalysts call the Oedipal victor. These children believe that they have prevailed over their fathers, having vanquished them from the home, and that their mothers are now solely theirs to enjoy. The state of being an Oedipal victor, however, has harmful effects on development. Boys who have not had an opportunity to bring the Oedipal conflict to a successful close tend to be fearful about their own aggressive impulses. They believe they are personally responsible for the departure of the father—and they tend to be greatly concerned about power issues. In many cases, the boys feel guilty about the divorce, blaming themselves for what happened, and consequently become quite timid and inhibited in adult life. An additional danger of not having a father with whom to identify may be homosexuality.

Young girls who do not experience a successfully resolved Electra complex may develop what psychoanalysts call a narcissistic mirror, in which they look to males for confirmation of their own sexuality. Because the girls did not have the experience of having their femininity confirmed by their fathers, they will engage in a fruitless search for identity through an endless series of sexual encounters. In the psychoanalytic view, the growing number of unresolved Electra complexes due to divorce is going to result in more promiscuity in the future. Ironically, psychoanalysts note, the independence that women achieve through divorce may lead to women's increased dependence on men for a sense of identity.

In the Soviet family—which will be dealt with in more detail later—divorce is also prevalent, and many children have grown up without significant interaction with their fathers. At the end of World War II, there were 20 million surplus women without husbands. Boris Kerblay attributes a loosening of moral standards in the postwar period to this surplus.

Although the divorce rate in the Soviet Union is about the same as in the United States, the reasons for divorce are different, with drunkenness on the part of the husband being cited as cause in almost 50 percent of all divorce cases in the Soviet Union. Interestingly, the Soviet people are not as inclined to remarry as Americans, with only 55 percent of the men and 70 percent of the women remarrying. Although the psychoanalytic view would hold that the Soviet divorce is just as harmful to the psychological development of children as the American divorce, the Soviet system has a different kind of socializing structure that, socialist theory holds, can make up for deficits within the family structure. This structure of political socialization and group activities may have arisen in response to the chronic lack of fathers in Soviet families since World War II. Furthermore, Soviet theorists reject psychoanalytic explanations for almost everything.

PSYCHOANALYSIS AND CAPITALISM

As suggested above, psychoanalysis as an explanation for human nature has only been viable within the capitalist cultures of the West. The hedonistic view of man the pleasure seeker found in psychoanalysis is consonant with the writings of the capitalist philosophers, and with Thomas Hobbes in particular. Going somewhat beyond the capitalist philosophers, however, Freud seemed to regard man as a kind of misanthrope, whose very unwilling participation in society is the price paid for survival. If it were possible, men would prefer to use others, including family members, only as outlets for their inborn sexual and aggressive instincts. Since these instincts cannot be expressed openly, they take sublimated forms in all areas of society. Freud was highly influenced by Darwin, and he seemed to regard life as a struggle in which the fit flourished while the weaker became neurotic.

Freud never believed that freedom is natural to men. Men are afraid of freedom—they realize that their instincts need controlling. For this reason men institute the kinds of oppressive governments and institutions that they feel they need. Although these governments exact a high price, they will keep human instincts under control. A secondary gain of repressive government is the offering of a flirtation with death. All governments, because they are by nature repressive, provide an outlet for what Erich Fromm has called the "necrophilous character"—an "attraction to all that is dead, decayed, putrid, sickly."

Whereas psychoanalysis and capitalism share a belief in the natural self-interestedness of men, they diverge on two other important points. First, Freud did not believe men acted on the basis of rational thinking. The unconscious is far too great a force for rational thought to control, and even when men appear to be acting on the basis of rational decisions, these decisions are colored by incidents from the first years of life. Freud believed that all life was symbolic—men have to fool themselves about their real motivations—so we can never take our actions at face value.

Second, Freud did not believe society ever really improved. The instincts are simply too powerful for technology, laws, or economic prosperity to subvert. There will never be a shortage of Nazis, Khmer Rouge, or Klan members—and Freud would in fact suggest that everyone has the potential for becoming members of these groups. Through most of Freud's later works—including Reflections on War and Death (1918), Beyond the Pleasure Principle (1920), Group Psychology and the Analysis of the Ego (1921), and Civilization and its Discontents (1930), Freud reaffirmed his belief that society is simply the product of mankind's collective unhappiness and neurosis. Because this unhappiness has an instinctual basis, substantive progress in human relations seems to be impossible.

Psychoanalysis has virtually nothing in common with socialist theory about the nature of man. Freud would have rejected totally the materialist interpretation of history, the notion that the essence of human life lies in social relations, and the belief that capitalism has any particular influence on human nature. Like capitalism, socialism is a melioristic theory, whereas psychoanalysis holds that individuals can never really improve themselves. No amount of self-improvement can ever give men what they really want.

In spite of some major differences, however, psychoanalytic theory does adhere to the capitalist belief that man is a self-interested creature who seeks to optimize his own pleasure. For whatever reason—man's intemperate nature or the evil of other men—man must be controlled, and hence governments are established at some cost to the individual. In his distaste for all ideologies and belief systems that obscure the true nature of life, however, Freud would have considered adherence to the world views of either capitalism or socialism to be a sure sign of neurosis.

EGO PSYCHOLOGY

The goal of the Freudian psychoanalytic psychotherapy is aptly summarized by Freud's famous remark that where there is id, "there shall ego be." Freud saw the id as that part of the mind that contained the most primitive biological drives. In addition to the sexual and death instincts, the drives for food, warmth, attention, and power are also in the id. When babies are born, they are all id. They do not temper their demands with reason but cry unceasingly for instant and complete gratification.

After some contact with the environment, however, babies begin to realize that they cannot always have their immediate wishes fulfilled and that strategies other than screaming may be more efficient in obtaining what they want. Screaming may in fact result in punishment. As babies unconsciously begin to recognize this fact, the ego starts to develop from the id. The ego has the difficult job of reconciling the demands of the id with the real world.

Freud never took much interest in the manner by which the ego mediates between the unreasonable and self-destructive demands of the id and the environment in which the person has to function. He was much more interested in the dark and seamy side of human nature and thus his principal writings focus on learning to control the id motivations.

In 1937, however, one year before Freud was forced by the Nazis to flee to London and two years before his death, Heinz Hartmann gave a series of lectures at the Vienna Psychoanalytic Society on the processes by which the ego adapts to the problems of everyday life. These lectures were published in 1939 in Hartmann's book, Ego Psychology and the Problem of Adaptation. This important work, first available in English in 1958, represents the first formal statement of ego psychology as well as the beginning of modern psychoanalysis' retreat from Freud's gloomy view of human nature.

Whereas Freud had stated that the ego develops from the traumatic struggle to control the id, Hartmann argued that the development of the ego is not so difficult a process. Under normal conditions, Hartmann suggested, the ego develops in a "conflict-free sphere." There is no dramatic struggle between ego and id, but rather the child's introduction to the expectations of society are relatively untraumatic. The ego comes with the genetic equipment to deal with what Hartmann called the "average expectable environment."

In modern psychoanalytic terms, the average expectable environment tends to mean the relationship between the mother and the child. Moving away from Freud's concern with controlling the destructive impulsives of the id, the ego psychologists have instead focused on those areas of the personality that are not governed by the id, such as intelligence, perception, creativity, and autonomy. Neurosis occurs when the ego has failed to develop the necessary mechanisms for dealing with the demands of everyday life. Very often, this failure to develop sufficient ego assets is the result of problems in the quality of the interaction between mother or primary caretaker and child. The psychoanalytic study of the quality of this interaction is called "object relations" or developmental psychoanalysis.

Object relations theorists generally believe that the child is born with the genetic equipment to make a reasonable adjustment to life, but that things often go wrong in the relationship between the child and its mother. Specifically, a mother may be cold, demanding, too busy, away from home too often, etc., and the child consequently develops a kind of insecurity. This insecurity translates into adult neurotic behavior such as excessive drinking, an inability to form satisfactory relationships with others, self-destructive impulses, or a lack of confidence. In contrast to Freud, who believed that a happy adjustment to life is genetically impossible, object relations theorists start with the premise that the child is born ready to adapt to the world as it is, but that something goes wrong along the way. Major object relations theorists include Anna Freud, Melanie Klein, Margaret Mahler, Otto Kernberg, Rene A. Spitz, and John Bowlby.

The second area within the broader field of ego psychology includes the psychoanalytic social psychologists, who take adaptation of the individual to his environment—as opposed to his relationship to his primary caretaker—as their point of departure. These include Karen Horney, Harry Stack Sullivan, Erik Erikson, and Erich Fromm. In the opinion of the social psychologists, neurosis is often more a product of maladaptation to the social system than it is in mother-child interaction. As in Erikson's example of the Sioux Indians, the quality of the relationship between the mother and the child was not nearly so problematical as fitting into modern, technological American culture. Fromm in particular has been a critic of capitalist culture, arguing that only a socialist society can offer the means for a full flowering of human nature. His ideas are discussed in the chapter on socialist humanism.

Although all ego psychologists are firm in their belief that they are moving psychoanalytic theory in the direction Freud would have chosen had he lived long enough, Freudian psychoanalysis and ego psychology have very different views of human nature. By removing the id from focus and concentrating instead on the ego, Hartmann and his followers have more or less jettisoned the unpleasant from psychoanalytic theory. Sexual and aggressive drives and the never-ending struggle with authority have been relegated to a minor role in human development. Rather than reconciling one's fear of castration by an omnipotent father, the most important tasks in life become having a good relationship with the caretaking mother during the first years of life, building a strong ego, and fitting into the culture into which one is born. If these tasks are successfully accomplished—which, by the way, ego psychologists find to be the case with virtually no one—the individual should have no particular problems adapting to the demands of ordinary life. Given the increasing number of absent mothers, however, both ego psychologists and orthodox analysts are pessimistic about the psychological adjustment of future generations.

Whereas Freudian psychoanalysis is actually a nihilistic theory that fits poorly with both the capitalist and socialist belief systems, ego psychology offers a set of beliefs that is congruent with many of the key propositions set forth by Adam Smith. The ego psychologists tend to believe that freedom or autonomy is natural to man and that self-interest is the primary motivating force in life. The baby enters into a social contract with his mother: he cooperates not because he wishes her beneficence, but because he needs her to get what he wants. From the relationship with his mother, he learns how to act with other people to get what he wants. He is not motivated by concern about the welfare of other human beings.

Ego psychologists accord man a far greater degree of rationality than Freud ever did. Since the ego is relatively free of destructive sexual and aggressiveness motives, it can look at the world in a realistic manner and not be subject to symbolic expression of the negative side of human nature. Because the normal individual has little problem keeping these drives under control, he can know meaning and satisfaction in his life in a way that Freud said was impossible. Also in agreement with the capitalist theorists, the ego psychologists believe that life can get better.

It is interesting to note that although many of the ego psychologists were born in Europe, most of their major theoretical contributions came after their emigration to the United States or England. Whereas orthodox Freudian analysts are relatively rare in modern capitalist cultures, ego psychology clearly dominates late twentieth-century psychoanalysis. The emphasis of the ego psychologists on the natural unfolding of the child's abilities, self-interest as the major motivation of human relationships, and adaptation to the environment in which one finds oneself makes their theories more compatible with a capitalist social structure than orthodox psychoanalysis could ever be.

Because humans are regarded as self-seeking misanthropes in all varieties of psychoanalysis (with the possible exception of Fromm's theory) psychoanalysis is clearly incompatible with Marxism. In spite of the efforts of such eminent psychoanalysts and economists as Erich Fromm and Robert Heilbroner to reconcile these two systems, this critical difference precludes any substantive synthesis.

Recognizing its incompatibility with socialism, the First All-Union Conference for the Study of Man's Behavior more or less exorcised psychoanalysis from the Soviet Union in 1930. Psychoanalysis in either its traditional or retooled version is still not well regarded in the Soviet Union and, according to the International Psychoanalytic Association, in all of Eastern Europe there are only 19 known analysts in Hungary and one in Czechoslovakia. Ego psychology as an explanation for human nature is clearly much more the product of capitalist, rather than socialist, culture.

7

Behaviorism

That's the source of the tremendous power of
positive reinforcement—there's no restraint and
no revolt. By a careful cultural design, we control not the final behavior, but the inclination to
behave, the motives, the desires, the wishes. The
curious thing is that in that case the question of
freedom never arises.

B. F. Skinner

Behaviorism, the most American of all explanations for human
nature, was born in the dog-bell-saliva studies of the great Russian
physiologist, Ivan Pavlov, and enjoyed widespread popularity in the
Soviet Union during the years immediately following the revolution.
The notion that people's actions can be explained by a particular stimulus that triggers specific responses has been profoundly appealing to
many American psychologists. Although Pavlov was interested in identifying the neural processes that give rise to behavior, American behaviorism later discarded altogether the role of the brain in behavior.
Instead, modern-day behaviorists have focused on the environment in
which behavior occurs. In the behaviorist framework, it is cues within
the environment that elicit behavior, and, some behaviorists argue,
individuals cannot be held responsible for the behaviors that those
cues elicit. This is held to be particularly true with regard to criminal behavior.

For example: during the Mariel boatlift of 1980, over 125,000
Cubans, some of them with records of serious crimes, entered the
United States during a six-month period that began in May of that year.
By October, all except 7,000 of the entrants had been released to spon-

sorships throughout the United States. Many of these remaining 7,000 had been somewhat arbitrarily categorized as being "antisocial" or "severely antisocial." They were concentrated in Fort Chaffee, just outside the town of Fort Smith, Arkansas, until the U.S. government could figure out what to do with them. Entrants whose crimes in Cuba were judged to be not too serious, however, were still eligible for traditional sponsorships by American families or church groups.

One entrant who had been serving a prison sentence in Cuba was offered a sponsorship by a charitable family of Americans and was sent to the Fort Smith airport to await a flight to his new home. After having experienced a rough life in Cuba, this individual was being offered a chance to make a new start. While the entrant waited for the plane, however, he decided to get some cash to help him with his new start by holding up the airport snack bar. The entrant was immediately caught, and in the ensuing commotion, needless to say, he lost his opportunity for becoming a self-reliant member of American society. He was shipped back to Fort Chaffee and from there to the Atlanta Federal Penetentiary, where federal officials tried to find a way to convince the Castro government to take him, and others like him, back.

Although the psychoanalytic explanation for such behavior would probably focus on aggressive drives and unresolved conflicts from early childhood, the behaviorist explanation is much simpler. Having probably grown up and certainly having spent several years in an environment where violent behavior is necessary for survival and the only way of accomplishing one's goals, the entrant was primed to respond to specific stimuli in an aggressive manner. The Fort Smith snack bar was small and isolated, operated by one female employee, and to the entrant it looked like an easy target for robbery. In other words, the stimuli coming from the situation triggered patterns of behavior for which the entrant had been rewarded throughout most of his life. It was the environment as much as the entrant that had caused the robbery.

It is this singular focus on the environment that makes American behaviorism the most materialistic of all personality theories, even more so than modern Soviet psychology. Not only are behaviorists hostile to such mentalistic and unverifiable notions as id, ego, or Oedipal conflict, they are hostile to any form of explanation that is not based on observable phenomena. Behaviorists regard the reliance upon concepts such as id motivations or death wishes to explain the behavior of the entrant in robbing the snack bar en route to his sponsorship as unscientific and superstitious. Nor do these theorists find using unobservable neural processes to explain behavior of much use either. According to classical behaviorists, in fact, there is no such thing as personality or human nature—there are only specific and limited instances of behavior.

The behaviorist asserts that we can explain behavior only by what we see. In 75 years of observation, research, and speculation, the behaviorist would point out, we have yet to see an id. Even with the unlikely possibility that the id does exist, the concept is not necessary to understand human behavior. In a manner reminiscent of Marx's emphasis on the world of human sensuous activity, the behaviorist believes that we must do away with mentalistic notions for which there is vague evidence and concentrate instead on the real world and the concrete acts of people within it. For this reason, "personality" is just as objectionable a notion as id—has anyone ever seen a personality? People are simply their behaviors, and attributing nonconcrete or even mystical concepts to an individual obscures the understanding or prediction of his or her behavior.

Our language is replete with these mentalistic "fictions," argues the eminent behaviorist, B. F. Skinner. What really happens in the world—and how we describe these events—are to him two quite different things. Consider Skinner's reinterpretation of the experiences of a college graduate who has been drafted:

> He lacks assurance or feels insecure or is unsure of himself (his behavior is weak and inappropriate); he is dissatisfied or discouraged (he is seldom reinforced, and as a result his behavior undergoes extinction); he is frustrated (extinction is accompanied by emotional responses); he feels uneasy or anxious (his behavior frequently has unavoidable aversive consequences which have emotional effects) . . . he is disappointed in himself and disgusted with himself (he is no longer reinforced by the admiration of others, and the extinction which follows has emotional effects); he becomes hypochondriacal (he concludes that he is ill) or neurotic (he engages in a variety of ineffective modes of escape); he experiences an identity crisis (he does not recognize the person he once called "I").

Maintaining a strict nonmentalistic, materialist outlook is a cornerstone of the behaviorist approach to understanding what has been referred to in this book as human nature or personality. In behaviorist parlance, for example, rats or people are never "hungry," since we cannot observe "hunger." They are merely "food-deprived." People are not "afraid" of snakes, they exhibit a fear response—drawing back or grimacing—when presented with a snake as a stimulus. In order to understand "human nature," behaviorists assert that we must keep our focus on observable behavior and discard (i.e., extinguish) our reliance on nonobservable, nonmeasurable concepts. During the 1970s, Skinner created a storm of protest by suggesting that concepts such as "freedom" and "dignity" are useless inventions that not only obscure, but actually prevent, the establishment of a world where everyone's basic needs can be met.

PAVLOV AND CLASSICAL CONDITIONING

Long before the revolution, Russian psychology had had a materialist base independent of the influence of Marx. The works of Lemonsov (1711-65), Mukhin (1766-1850), Dyad'kovskii (1784-1841), Filomafitskii (1807-49), and Sechenov (1829-1905) were all concerned with understanding the relationship between neural activities and physiological activities and behavior.

Pavlov (1849-1936), whose work with the glandular and neural functioning in digestion won him a Nobel Prize in 1904, is known in Western psychology as the founder of classical conditioning, the immediate predecessor to behaviorism. Pavlov called his discovery of the process by which organisms make neural connections between unrelated phenomena such as bells and meat the "conditioned reflex."

From his early work with dogs, Pavlov went on to formulate hypotheses about human development, and by 1928, Soviet scientists were engaged in attempting to condition humans to salivate at the proper stimulus. Pavlov suggested that when a child is born, he has a few basic reflexes that, over time, are paired with a wide variety of stimuli, so that eventually all instances of behavior are packages of conditioned reflexes derived from the inherited reflexes. Pavlov's psychology was pure physiology: a given adult smiles frequently not because he is friendly, but because stimuli in his adult environment activate the neural connections that led to his smiling at an earlier stage of development. The environment itself is not nearly so important as the physical make-up of the individual's brain.

Pavlov thought that all behaviors could be traced to conditioned reflexes—neural impulses that had become associated with specific stimuli—and that one had only to discover the areas of the brain that were affected by these impulses. Although the reflexes the child starts with may be very simple, the behaviors that eventually develop can be amazingly complex. In a statement that must have chagrined the Bolshevik government, Pavlov even went so far as to assert that Anglo-Saxons have an inherited "reflex of purpose" that is lacking in Russians.

Nevertheless, Pavlov was at first highly regarded by the Bolshevik government. On January 24, 1921, Lenin signed a special decree providing government support for Pavlov's work. The party considered Pavlov to be a "spontaneous materialist"—one who came to a materialist understanding of history without studying philosophy—and it was felt that Pavlov could eventually provide empirical physiological evidence for Marxist theory. For political reasons that will be discussed later, however, the work of Pavlov, just as American behaviorism, fell out of favor in the Soviet Union in the 1930s.

JOHN B. WATSON AND LITTLE ALBERT

John B. Watson (1878-1958) is considered the founder of American behaviorism. Although his early work ignored Pavlov and classical conditioning, Watson later became a major proponent of the conditioning approach to understanding human behavior. In his 1908 paper, "Psychology as the behaviorist views it," Watson introduced the ideas that form the basis of all later behavioristic conceptions about human "personality." The goal of behaviorism, wrote Watson, is simply the prediction and control of behavior. There is no reason why people and animals should be studied in different ways, and consciousness, ostensibly the great divider that separates man from ape, is a useless, if not meaningless, concept.

Watson believed that all complex adult emotional reactions were the product of the pairing of various stimuli with the three fundamental emotions found in infants: fear, rage, and love. In a famous series of experiments at Johns Hopkins University in 1920, Watson and his assistant, Rosalie Raynor, attempted to demonstrate how emotions are merely the product of conditioning.

Little Albert was a nine-month old infant selected as the subject for the experiment. Using the principles of behaviorism, Watson and Raynor were intent on introducing a phobia into an otherwise healthy infant and seeing if that phobia would transfer to other phenomena. Specifically, Watson and Raynor wanted to induce a phobia of white rats in Little Albert, then see if this phobia would then generalize to similar objects.

In the experiment, Little Albert initially showed no fear when he was presented with a white rat. When he touched the white rat, however, an assistant would strike a metal bar with a hammer, producing a loud, unpleasant clanging sound that was known to "frighten"—i.e., produce a fear response—in Albert. After seven pairings of the rat and the clanging, Albert began to cry whenever the rat was presented without the noise. In addition to the rat, Albert eventually appeared to show a fear response when presented with a variety of furry objects— a rabbit, dog, sealskin coat, a bearded Santa Claus mask, and Watson's hair. The experiments with Little Albert ended about a month later when his mother removed him from the hospital where the experiment had been conducted.

In later experiments with different children, Watson and his assistants worked at inducing a fear response, then eliminating it. This was done by conditioning a child to fear a rabbit, then later introducing

the rabbit into the far end of the room while the child was eating. Over
several sessions the rabbit was introduced closer and closer to the
subject, until eventually the child could handle the rabbit without exhibiting a fear response. Watson was satisfied that through the principles of behaviorism he had uncovered the scientific basis for human
emotion.

Unfortunately, Watson's scientific career came to a premature
close as a result of a divorce scandal culminating in his marrying
Raynor and being asked to resign from Hopkins. Watson left academics
altogether and joined the advertising firm of J. Walter Thompson where
he applied the principles of behaviorism to marketing. One of Watson's
accounts was Scott Tissue, where he used the aversive stimulus of the
threat of disease to frighten people into buying Scott toilet paper:

> Watson's Scott Tissue campaign warned that harsh toilet
> papers caused irritation that "is not only a source of dis-
> comfort but also a possible seat of infection." One adver-
> tisement showed a photograph of a woman lying despondent
> in a hospital bed, a concerned friend hovering at her side;
> another showed a team of surgeons preparing to operate
> on a hapless victim of harsh paper.

In spite of his premature departure from academics, however,
Watson had set the stage for the development of the second great
school—psychoanalysis being the first—of psychological personality
theory, behaviorism.

In Watsonian behaviorism, there is no such thing as human nature. People are neither good nor evil nor acquisitive nor anything
that they are not conditioned to be. Aside from physiological features,
humans come into the world more or less as blank slates. It is the
combination of factors in the environment that shape those behaviors
that individual adopts and that the less scientifically-minded call personality. All people are essentially the same at birth, and within the
limits of physiology, all people can become all things. In an often-
quoted statement, Watson claimed:

> Give me a dozen healthy infants, well-formed, and my
> own specified world to bring them up in, and I'll guaran-
> tee to take any one at random and train him to become
> any type of specialist I might select—a doctor, lawyer,
> artist, merchant-chief and yes, even into a beggar-man
> and thief, regardless of his talents, penchants, tenden-
> cies, abilities, vocations and race of his ancestors.

Given that individuals are simply the product of their respective
environments, Watson argued that individuals cannot be held account-

able for their actions. Individuals become criminals because of their environments, and they don't deserve to be punished—they need to be reeducated by being taught desirable behavior. This approach was particularly appealing to the Bolsheviks, who felt that the natural "goodness" of the Russian people had been corrupted by living in an oppressive czarist society, and Watsonian behaviorism was for a time very popular in the Soviet Union. In 1927, Watson contributed an article on behaviorism in The Great Soviet Encyclopedia.

THE APPEAL OF BEHAVIORISM

While psychoanalysis has been extremely influential in such areas as literature, political science, and anthropology, it is behaviorism that has dominated twentieth-century American academic psychology. In the United States, behaviorism has been far more popular than it has been anywhere else in the world. The reasons for this appeal are several. First, the techniques of behaviorism are simple: one brings about change in behavior through reinforcement. Identifying the proper reinforcements and developing a schedule for their application may require some sophistication, but the basic principles are easy to comprehend. Behaviorism requires no protracted study of unconscious motivations, defense mechanisms, or Oedipal conflicts.

Second, the focus of behaviorism readily lends itself to the prevailing method of psychology—the experiment—in a way that psychoanalysis cannot. Behavior is observable and measurable and one can see results in trying to manipulate it. Psychoanalytic insight, on the other hand, is virtually unmeasurable and, as any psychoanalyst will concede, is no guarantee of a change in behavior. Use of the scientific method in studying behavior also puts psychology on a presumably equal methodological footing with physics, chemistry, and the other natural sciences.

Third, behaviorists can demonstrate remarkable achievements through the use of the principles of reinforcement. While years of psychoanalytic psychotherapy may lead to almost no change in a person's behavior or psychological state, behaviorist techniques can often bring about abrupt change. In a fascinating report of the effectiveness of behavior modification techniques, Irene Kassorla described how a catatonic schizophrenic who had been mute for 30 years was taught to speak.

In 30 years, the only words the patient had spoken were "ugh" and something that sounded like "crack 'em." In the first stage of the experiment, the patient was rewarded with food every time he attempted to say "crack 'em." In a later stage, the patient was shown a picture of a dog and given food when he repeated the word "dog," but only praised when he said "crack 'em."

This procedure was repeated with other objects, until after 31 days the formerly mute patient could name 150 objects correctly. At that point, the experimenters began to take the patient outside the hospital grounds and introduce new words to him, giving him food each time he made a correct identification. In order to make him independent of continual reinforcement, however, the patient was eventually rewarded intermittently rather than regularly. At the end of 138 days, the patient was able to ask questions and talk, albeit in a somewhat unspontaneous manner, with other patients. After 30 years of silence, the patient had learned to talk and was no longer catatonic.

Finally, behaviorism lends itself to an optimistic view of the future in a way that psychoanalysis could never do. Freud himself was convinced that psychoanalysis could never affect the future—that it was destined always to be a retrospective activity designed to undo the damage of infantile trauma. Behaviorism, on the other hand, offered a method that could shape the future to create any kind of world—or any kind of personality—that humanity desired. In a review of Watson's 1925 book, Behaviorism, the New York Herald Tribune commented, "Perhaps this is the most important book ever written. One stands for a moment blinded with a great hope."

BEHAVIORISM AND TELEVISION

Although Watson and Skinner used the concept of reinforcement to explain how people learn, psychologist Albert Bandura in 1963 introduced experimental evidence that children can learn simply by observing behavior and without reinforcement. Using a television set with either real people or a cartoon cat showing violent behavior, Bandura demonstrated that children watching the set became more violent without receiving any reinforcement for violent actions. From Bandura's perspective, children can learn behaviors simply by observation. Since the average American child or adult spends 25 to 30 hours per week watching television (in contrast to 9-10 hours for Soviet males and 4-5 hours for Soviet females), observational learning theorists would predict that American children are likely to be learning to do what they see on the screen. And since some theorists have suggested that American children are no longer being raised by their parents but more often by their teachers and by television, it is important to take a look at the effects of television viewing on the socialization of American children.

In fact, average American children now spend about twice as much time watching television as they do in school. By the time a child graduates from high school, he or she will have seen approximately 22,000 hours of television, compared with the 11,000 spent actually in the classroom. By the age of six months, American babies are estimated to be watching an hour of television per day. According to the National Institute of Mental Health report Television and Behavior, television features an average of 5 violent acts per prime time hour and 18 violent acts per hour during children's weekend programs. It has been estimated that by the time a child reaches 16 years of age, he or she will have witnessed 18,000 murders on the television.

According to the NIMH report, the causal link between television and violence is now quite clear:

> After more than 10 years of research, the consensus among most of the research community is that violence on television does lead to aggressive behavior by children and teenagers who watch the programs. . . . Children who watch a lot of violence on television may come to accept violence as normal behavior.

Researchers feel that television is a "major socializing agent of American children," where children learn about people and life. As a socializing agent, however, the fantasy world of television is seldom reflective of real life. For example, male characters on the television tend to be universally strong, manly, and somewhat older than the females. Women, on the other hand, are portrayed as being stereotypically passive and feminine. In contrast to real life, almost 70 percent of the women on television don't work. Television jobs tend to be higher status except in the case of women and minority characters, and relatively few major characters hold blue-collar positions. Whereas blacks account for about 10 percent of the characters on television, there are virtually no Hispanics, Native Americans, or Asian Americans. Although television still contains many of the prototypical families of working father/homemaking mother and children, divorced and single parents, as well as unmarried couples living together, have become more prevalent.

With regard to the use of alcohol, the average child sees 10 episodes of drinking daily, totaling some 3,000 episodes in a year's time. In contrast to smokers, who are relatively rare on television now and who tend to be unlikeable characters, drinkers are generally good, likeable, and fun. During prime time, children are likely to see 12 doctors and 6 nurses every week. About 90 percent of these doctors are white males who are always depicted as being more personable and smarter than the nurses. In keeping with the general unreality of television, television doctors spend 61 percent of their time making house calls.

American television, where the average child sees 22,000 commercials yearly, also teaches children to consume:

Research shows that consumer roles are learned from television. Children are taught to be avid consumers; they watch the commercials, they ask their parents to buy the products, and they use or consume the products. . . .

Game shows with money and other prizes display explicit consumer behavior. The ecstasy of the winners and the studio audience's appreciative applause probably engender desires for consumer goods among the viewers.

From a behaviorist perspective, television is shaping the behaviors of our children, and it is not surprising that, in a capitalist society, commercialism would be one of the major lessons drawn from television viewing. In contrast to many other societies, American television is a medium for marketing first and a source for entertainment or education second. (An Arab immigrant once informed me that "Dallas" is shown in Iraq, prefaced by a message about how the following program shows the decadence and deleterious effects of capitalism.)

Another cultural value taught by television is competition. In an interesting study of the content of children's television, media specialist Earle F. Barcus found that the major theme expressed in children's programming is competition and rivalry between characters.

Television's emphasis on violence, on the other hand, is somewhat less easy to explain. Although Americans tend not to think of themselves as violent people, statistics suggest otherwise. Marvin Harris has pointed out, for example, that there are 5 times more homicides, 10 times more rapes, and 17 times more robberies in the United States than in Japan. Whatever the attraction, violence sells, and the NIMH report concludes that the link between violence on television and violence on the street is indisputable.

Bandura's findings about the persuasive power of television present a sobering picture of the future when considered in light of present-day television fare. Behaviorists such as Skinner argue that although we now have sufficiently sophisticated technology—such as television—to make real progress in shaping human behavior, that technology is inefficiently used. Whereas television may be making an important cultural contribution by teaching highly regarded values such as consumerism, it seems likely that the emphasis on violence may be having the opposite effect.

BEHAVIORIST PERSONALITY

In spite of the widespread enthusiasm of some personality psychologists for behaviorism, the concept of personality is still anathema to most behaviorists. Although behaviorists do not deny the existence of inner drives or genetic capabilities, they consider these to be less important than factors in the environment. Given the proper schedules of reinforcement, individuals can be raised to exhibit socialist, capitalist, anarchist, or any other kinds of behaviors, regardless of the system into which they are born. Given the proper reinforcement, anyone can become anything. Inherent personal qualities of people such as Plato, Napoleon, Kafka, or Lindbergh cannot explain their achievements. Rather, their achievements are products of the reinforcements they received throughout their lives. In contrast to the psychoanalytic view that personality or behavior is fairly set at the end of the Oedipal period (ages 3-5), behaviorists believe that proper reinforcement, as in the case of Kassorla's catatonic schizophrenic, can change an individual at any time.

People are neither rational nor irrational in the behaviorist framework. They can be conditioned to be mercenaries or great humanitarians. They can learn to be consumers or aesthetes. People can be taught to approach the world in a purely emotional manner, or they can be conditioned to face the world with pure logic. Particulars in Gandhi's life influenced him to become a pacifist (exhibit pacifistic behaviors); Lenin's experience led him to believe in armed struggle. Contingencies in the life of Virginia Woolf led to a career in literature—but reinforcements were not sufficient to maintain her desire to live. Whatever behaviors an individual demonstrates are traceable to reinforcements within the environment of that individual.

Are people cooperative or competitive? Again, people can be anything that their environments encourage them to be. The use of proper technology in environmental design makes the achievement of any personality type well within the realm of possibilities. The behaviorist, while rejecting the use of such ostensibly prescientific terms as "roles" as it has been used in this book, would nevertheless readily agree with the basic premise of this book—that people are what their environments teach them to be and behaviors appropriate to one environment won't necessarily be appropriate in another. The reason why some people fail to cooperate with the capitalist or socialist systems is that those systems are inefficiently designed, not that people are naturally cooperative or competitive. Aside from being subject to their physiological drives, people are not naturally anything.

With regard to faulty design of the environment, Skinner makes the point that while technology has experienced amazing growth since the time of the Greeks, the science of behavior has not:

> Aristotle could not have understood a page of modern
> physics or biology, but Socrates and his friends would
> have little trouble in following most current discussions

of human affairs. And as to technology, we have made immense strides in controlling the physical and biological worlds, but our practices in government, education, and much of economics though adapted to very different conditions, have not greatly improved. . . . Whereas Greek physics and biology, no matter how crude, led eventually to modern science, Greek theories of human behavior led nowhere.

That is to say, the science of understanding human behavior is hardly less primitive today than it was in the time of the Greeks. What the world needs to provide for the physical and psychological needs of its peoples, the behaviorists argue, is the discarding of concepts such as freedom and dignity and a redirection of effort toward building a controlled environment where people can be taught how to behave in the best interests of everyone. The technology for building that world has almost been achieved, but the clinging to unscientific notions about human nature has forestalled its establishment.

BEHAVIORISM AND IDEOLOGY

Unlike Freudian psychoanalysis, which fits in poorly with either capitalist or socialist ideologies, behaviorist explanations for human nature fit in well with both. The behaviorist approach to understanding personality and behavior allows its techniques to be applied in any kind of society. One simply designs a schedule of reinforcement that results in capitalist or socialist behavior in order to create the kind of personality desired. In the Soviet Union and the United States, the institutions are designed, although in ineffective and unscientific manners, to create those kinds of reinforcements, and consequently shape behavior.

Nevertheless, the initial enthusiasm for behaviorism in the Soviet Union waned with the promulgation of the Soviet Constitution of 1936. At that time Stalin declared that the Soviet Union had reached its goal of achieving socialism. According to Marxist theory, the establishment of a socialist society would allow people to express their natural instincts toward cooperation. In that the Soviet Union in 1936 still had problems with antisocial and counterrevolutionary elements, it was decided that the ostensibly socialist environment could not be held responsible for these problems. Behaviorism, with its emphasis on the environment and denial of individual responsibility, was seen as being too limited to be useful in understanding the psychology of individuals. For this same reason, the popularity of Pavlovian classical conditioning also declined.

An additional problem with behaviorism was its methodology:

Marxist theorists have had some problems in reconciling the experimental method with the dialectic. The problem of the method of behaviorism is discussed in Chapter 12.

It is interesting to note how popular behaviorism is in the United States, the most capitalist of all societies, in spite of a number of conflicts between these two ideologies. Behaviorists assert that the environment in which people live must be strictly controlled, which is totally at odds with the capitalist notion of autonomous man. Whereas supply-side economics apotheosizes autonomous man, Skinner cannot wait to be free of him:

> Autonomous man is a device used to explain what we cannot explain in any other way. He has been constructed from our ignorance, and as our understanding increases, the very stuff of which he is composed vanishes. . . . To man qua man we readily say good riddance. Only by dispossessing him can we turn to the real causes of human behavior. Only then can we turn from the inferred to the observed, from the miraculous to the natural, from the inaccessible to the manipulable.

In addition to their hostility toward autonomy, behaviorists don't take kindly to the concept of individual responsibility. As Watson argued, since behavior is the product of conditions in the environment, how can we hold the individual personally responsible for what he has been reinforced to do? In further contrast to capitalist theory, behaviorists do not see society as oppressive. Rather, what is needed is more society, more planning, more control over the lives of individuals and their personal experiences. Vague concepts as freedom, dignity, or the sanctity of the free enterprise system have not advanced the course of human history. People today are just as mean-spirited and capable of destruction as they were in the time of Attila the Hun, except that now they have nuclear warheads and Saturday-night specials rather than spears and arrows at their disposal. The behavior of individuals is going to have to be shaped toward different goals if the world is to survive.

In spite of these contradictions, there are a number of reasons for behaviorism's continuing popularity in the United States. First, behaviorism is the most purely American of all personality theories. Although classical conditioning is regarded as the intellectual predecessor to behaviorism, it is the American proponents of the conditioning approach that have raised behaviorism to a sophisticated and widely applied psychology. Operant conditioning and social learning, the two varieties of behaviorism presently most influential, are purely American in origin.

Another way in which behaviorism is congruent with a capitalist belief system is in its melioristic view of the future. Skinner and other behaviorists are confident that their approach can create utopias. While capitalists regard progress as inevitable, behaviorists would suggest only that it can be, given the proper structuring of environment. Orthodox psychoanalysts, on the other hand, would scoff at the idea of progress.

Behaviorism depends on technology in the same way that capitalism depends upon technology, and behaviorist principles are used to promote efficiency in learning just as the entrepreneur attempts to promote efficiency on the assembly line. Both ideologies share the belief that science and a rational approach to life are the keys to any kind of progress.

Finally, behaviorism is pragamatic in a way that nihilistic psychoanalysis can never be. This pragmatism is probably the major reason why behaviorism fits in so well with the capitalist business system. In the behaviorist framework, as in the business system, one identifies one's goals and attempts to move toward them in as rational a fashion as possible. Whether these goals be increasing a market share or teaching a catatonic schizophrenic to speak, the procedures for accomplishment are the same: identify one's objectives, design a plan for achieving them, and measure one's outcome to see if the objective has been attained. Probably the greatest American contribution to economic theory is the development of the principles of marketing, which are very much influenced by behavioristic ideas about human nature and shaping behavior.

In behaviorism, as in capitalism, the preferred method or treatment plan is the one that works. This emphasis on results over theory, so intrinsic to both behaviorism and U.S. business culture, is probably the most compelling reason why behaviorism continues to be the most popular explanatory model for human nature in American psychology.

8

The New Soviet Man

> We want to build socialism with the aid of those
> men and women who grew up under capitalism,
> were depraved and corrupted by capitalism, but
> steeled for the struggle by capitalism. . . . We
> want to start building socialism at once out of the
> material that capitalism left us yesterday to be
> used today, at this very moment, and not with
> people reared in hothouses.

Lenin

The purpose of the October Revolution was to do away with the
repressive precapitalist czarist society and replace it with the kind
of humane socialism where all the lost traits of human nature could
again become manifest. But because the Russian people had suffered
under the czarist system for so long and were so backward and igno-
rant, the Bolsheviks felt that they could not immediately be trusted to
understand what was involved in the establishment and maintenance of
a socialist government in a hostile capitalist world. Lenin believed
that it was the role of the Party to provide the Russian people with the
kind of leadership they needed until they could regain those qualities
of cooperation and self-actualization that Marx had described.

But the Russian people were not like the British or German industrial workers who were at least allowed some degree of political
participation, however slight. Although the serfs had been freed in
1861, the highly bureaucratic central government still owned most of
the land and industry and employed most of the people. Social stratification kept peasants and industrial workers legally segregated from

other social groups. Censorship precluded any discussion of political issues, and the vast network of secret police searched for revolutionaries throughout the society. Further, the extravagance of the government had necessitated heavy borrowing from the West, so that the czar was often more subject to the wishes of his foreign creditors than to those of his people at home.

The question of the ability of a people removed from the dark ages by less than 60 years to establish and maintain a socialist government was more than a matter of dealing with ignorance and lack of education. As Lenin and the Bolsheviks consolidated their power toward the end of the civil war (1918-20), it became obvious that while reform would be used whenever possible, it was actually a new kind of person that was needed for carrying out the goals of the revolution and the establishment of a Marxist state. The new kind of person was to be the embodiment of the natural state of man as Marx had envisioned him before he became corrupted by capitalism and the feudalism that precedes capitalism. Toward the end of the civil war, party officials turned increasingly to psychologists and educators for ideas about how to teach the people and how to return them to the persons they would have been before the rise of capitalism.

One of the new Soviet men (actually a Soviet boy) created by the revolution was a martyr by the name of Pavlik Morozov, whose memory is enshrined today in a statue in Moscow. Schoolchildren from all over the Soviet Union visit this statue in order to pay homage to his memory. Pavlik was a member of the Soviet youth group, the Pioneers, during the period of collectivization in the 1920s. Pavlik's father did not believe in the Bolshevik cause and was engaged in counterrevolutionary activity. Pavlik reported him to the Bolshevik authorities for collaborating with the Kulaks, the wealthy landowners who were resisting collectivization. Further, young Morozov testified for the prosecution against his father in court. When he returned home from the trial, the angry villagers killed Pavlik in vengeance for betraying the Kulak cause and for testifying against his father. The story of his martyrdom is held up to Soviet schoolchildren as an example of the kind of self-sacrifice necessary to accomplish the goals of establishing an egalitarian communist state.

Loyalty to abstract notions such as state or party is not unknown in the United States, but rarely does it reach such a degree that informing on one's father is a behavior that is rewarded by anyone. The Bolsheviks, however, were creating a new society for which new rules had to be forged and for which all kinds of extreme behaviors were justifiable. The Soviet attempt to develop a new kind of psychology for creating a new kind of a person is an event whose significance is not generally appreciated in the West. Never had social science been given such an important task. The not uncommon view of Soviet psychology as brainwashing or totalitarianism is a simplistic approach to understanding a tradition that stands on firmer philosophical grounds than most Western psychologies. The Bolsheviks had destroyed the past and given science the mandate to create a new kind of person.

A. S. MAKARENKO

By the end of 1919, the Soviet government had gained military control of the Ukraine, and in September 1920 the authorities asked a young schoolteacher by the name of A. S. Makarenko to establish a school at Poltava for wayward children. Years of war, revolution, civil war, and invasion by forces from the capitalist nations had wreaked a terrible toll in human lives in the Soviet Union. Aside from the estimated 9.7 million Russians who died during this period, there were uncountable numbers of orphans left to their own devices for survival. Many of these children became criminals at very early ages, and they presented a special kind of problem for the revolutionary committees. Makarenko's school at Poltava was organized around the reeducation of these wayward youths into model Soviet citizens.

Makarenko's first six inmates were between the ages of 16 and 18 and they had been convicted of such crimes as housebreaking, armed robbery, and manslaughter. As might be expected, they were hostile, insolent, and dangerous. For the first few months after the opening of the school, the "students" used their new home as a base for their criminal activities. Makarenko, who had been trained in elementary education, at first did not know what to do about these activities. Finally, in a famous incident reminiscent of Helen Keller and Anne Sullivan at the water pump, Makarenko had an insight that allowed him to gain control of the situation. He had asked Zadorov, one of the students, to chop wood for the school. When Zadorov refused, Makarenko, who had been a patient teacher for several months, lost his temper:

> That was the first time any of the boys addressed me
> with such disrespect. Desperate with rage and indig-
> nation, driven to utter exasperation by the experiences
> of the previous months, I raised my hand and dealt
> Zadorov a blow full in the face. I hit him so hard that
> he lost his balance and fell against the stove. Again I
> struck him, seizing him by the collar and actually lift-
> ing him on his feet. And then I struck him the third time.

Zadorov was one of the worst lawbreakers, and Makarenko was literally risking his own life by attacking him. The outcome was not surprising, however, given the environments from which the boys had come. Having grown up in a world where violence was the only way of achieving any kind of respect from others, Zadorov responded favorably to Makarenko's beating. Without a further word, Zadorov picked up the axe and went outside to chop the wood.

Word of the incident spread through the colony, and it was the beginning of a new cooperation on the part of the inmates. From this incident Makarenko got an insight that was to be critically influential in Soviet thinking about education and psychology in the following decades. The theories and methods learned from the literature on education of that period were virtually useless in dealing with the extraordinary situation of reeducating youth made criminal by war and revolution. Makarenko realized that an entirely new kind of education would have to be developed to deal with the kind of person that the revolution had left in its wake. This new education would have to come from real world experience and not mere academic theorizing.

INTERPRETING MARXIST PSYCHOLOGY

In many respects, having an official ideology such as Marxism to which scientific works must conform makes life simpler for the scientist. Problems arise, however, when this ideology is capable of being interpreted in more ways than one. A broad and sweeping theory of human nature, history, and economics such as Marxism leaves many areas open to differing interpretations of data. During the 1920s, Soviet academics and party theorists debated many issues relevant to the role of Marxism and both the natural and physical sciences. During this period, Pavlov's classical conditioning and related schools of neuropsychology were so prestigious and highly regarded by party members that psychologists found themselves struggling to justify the existence of their field. The two most influential researchers in human behavior at that time, Pavlov and Bekhterev, the founder of reflexology, were hostile to psychology and dissociated themselves entirely from the field.

As suggested in the last chapter, however, the problem of free will and individual responsibility—which, by the way, is not a materialist conception—provided a means for psychology to return to favor in the 1920s. Since the concept of free will became necessary to explain the behavior of individuals who acted in their own interests and contrary to the perceived interests of society, psychology enjoyed something of a renaissance toward the end of the decade. Further, social scientists were still struggling with new approaches toward creating the new Soviet man, and educational and industrial psychology became important areas of research. Even psychoanalysis, with its emphasis on sexuality and the unconscious, was popular with some Soviet psychologists.

At the First All-Union Conference for the Study of Man's Behavior in 1930, scientists agreed that there was more to human behavior than reflexes, and that the environment played the most important part in the development of human behavior. In addition to criticizing Pavlovian views on human behavior, Freudian psychology was also dismissed as being too deterministic and too focused on the past. In her memoirs of Lenin published in 1925, Clara Zetkin had reported that Lenin had never been comfortable with Freud's preoccupation with sex, and in his autobiography, Trotsky had commented that, with regard to psychoanalysis, "much in this field is still vague and unstable and opens the way for fanciful and arbitrary ideas."

The All-Union Conference of 1930 was a milestone in Soviet psychology because it introduced several new approaches to understanding personality that had previously been considered incompatible with Marxism. First, purely materialistic reflex theories were criticized because they were too narrow. There had to be a means of accounting for free will. Taking a step back from the materialism of Marx, members of the conference decided that there had to be something analogous to a "psyche" or mind that allowed individuals to make decisions. The study of the psyche was to be the province of psychology, not physiology, and all researchers were to continue in their efforts to develop information that would be helpful in creating the new Soviet man. The new information was, of course, to be consistent with Marxist theory.

PEDOLOGICAL PERVERSIONS OF 1936

During the 1930s, official attitudes toward psychology were colored by political events. Psychological testing, which had always been popular, became extremely fashionable early in the decade. The measurement of intelligence, personnel testing, and personality assessment were all widely used at the beginning of the decade, in spite of the fact that the tests overall were poorly constructed, lacked reliability and validity, and incompetently administered.

Toward the middle of the decade, however, psychology began to fall into disfavor. Widespread use of psychological testing had revealed patterns of behavior that were inconsistent with Marxist theory and had shown that tests favored certain groups, allowing them to score higher than other groups (a fact that would not be seriously considered in the West for another 30 years). Intelligence testing and personnel selection procedures were criticized for perpetuating class differences. Measurement study of attitudes was forbidden because people were found to have "chauvinistic" opinions about the government: they were not as enthusiastic about collectivization as the government would have liked. Worst of all, party members often scored lower on psychological tests than nonmembers.

On July 4, 1936, the Central Committee issued its paper, "Concerning Pedological Perversions in the Systems of the People's Commissariat of Education," which severely criticized both educational psychology—known as pedology—and psychological testing as instruments for perpetuating class differences. Because Stalin had asserted in the Constitution of 1936 that the Soviet Union had achieved its goal of establishing a socialist society, the two-factor theory of behavior as solely the product of heredity and environment was no longer acceptable. Two-factor theory was ruled out because the production of antisocial personalities in a socialist society was logically impossible. Henceforth character was to be thought of as the product of the three factors of heredity, environment, and vospitaniye, or training at school and at home. Although environment was still considered important in the development of personality, training was clearly to be the area of study in the future. Psychologists were further directed to spend less time on academic study and more time on research that would help in developing good Soviet citizens. The entire field of industrial psychology—psychotechnics—was virtually abolished, and an emphasis on training in the work place became paramount.

In 1938, N. K. Kornilov, using extensive references to Marxist-Leninist classics, published his paper on "correct" positions in psychology. The proper role of psychology was further defined in R. L. Rubinshtein's Foundations of General Psychology in 1940. The positions outlined by Kornilov and Rubinshtein have generally dominated the study of psychology in the Soviet Union until the present day.

SOCIALIZING THE NEW SOVIET MAN

One of the major ideas of this book is that societies are structured to raise the kind of personality necessary for maintenance of the system, and certainly the Soviet Union is no different in this respect. While American child-rearing practices clearly emphasize independence and consumerism, Soviet child rearing has group affiliation and devotion to duty as its goal.

In contrast to the American emphasis on independence, psychologist Urie Bronfenbrenner has observed that one of the major goals of Soviet upbringing is to teach children to be obedient to authority. Bronfenbrenner suggests that the most striking feature of parent-child relationships in the Soviet Union is its "emotional loading"—the extreme (by American standards) demonstrativeness by Soviet parents toward their children and the extreme withdrawal of affection which is used as punishment for misbehavior.

Although the Bolshevik system initially encouraged placement of children in nurseries to get them away from "chauvinistic" attitudes on the part of their parents, current Soviet policy allows parental influence to be paramount during the first six years of life. Working Soviet women receive two months leave with pay prior to a birth, as well as two months paid leave after the birth. Should the birth be difficult or twins, the woman is allowed an extra month off. Part-time leave is available until the child is one year old; at the end of the first year the mother can take an additional year of unpaid leave.

Although children can be placed in public nurseries at three months, only 10 percent of Soviet children under two years are so placed. During the first year of life in the nursery, Bronfenbrenner reports, children are kept together in playpens with six to eight other children. These playpens are raised so as to allow face-to-face interaction with caretaking adults. When children are placed in the nursery, working mothers are allowed one half hour off for every three and a half hours worked in order to visit their children.

In contrast to the allegedly nondoctrinaire approach of Western schools, the Soviet educational system has the specific mission of installing socialist values. As Boris Kerblay commented:

The moral code places the highest value on the positive virtues such as fatherland, Lenin, socialism, work, study, solidarity; all virtues encouraging the sacrifice of personal desires to the interests of the group, respect for the Party, devotion to the welfare of the people, and defence of the oppressed peoples of the world. Negative values are personified by imperialism, capitalists and the exploiters and speculators of the old regime.

In grades one through three, all Soviet children are members of a group called the Octobrists, which is an organization designed to instill vospitaniye and love for the collective in its members. Laws of the Octobrists require a positive attitude toward school, respect for grown-ups, an enjoyment of work, honesty and truthfulness, and good friendship. Competition between Octobrists is never individualized, but rather between schools, classrooms, or rows within a classroom. Because all activity is done in groups, children are socialized to put group values ahead of individual values. These values are reinforced in two other student groups, the Pioneers (grades four through eight) and the Komsomol (grade nine up to age 28). Whereas membership in the Octobrists and Pioneers is universal, only one-third of the eligible children join the Komsomol.

The task of the Komsomol, an organization of 35 million young adults that has no counterpart in American society, is to organize the most politically active youth into a community that political scientist John N. Hazard characterizes as being "second only to the Communist

Party itself." From this corps of volunteers future party members are recruited, but the Komsomol has fulfilled other important functions in society. In the 1920s they built the city of Komsomolsk in the Far East, and in the 1930s Komsomol members worked on building the Moscow subway. In recent years they have served in construction projects from the Arctic Circle to Central Asia.

As suggested above, the Soviet system of education socializes children to Marxist-Leninist values. Since these values are the only permissible ideals to which children can aspire, deviance from the Marxist line tends to bring punishment or ostracism. Throughout the Soviet system, children are taught to sacrifice their personal betterment for the betterment of the collective, to obey authority, and to devote themselves to the abstract goals of socialist revolution. The individualism that is taught in U.S. schools is regarded as decadence in Soviet schools; the Soviet emphasis on children's obedience to authority is seen as totalitarianism in the West.

THE NEW SOVIET MAN TODAY

Although Soviet psychology has attempted to remain faithful to the teachings of Marx, Engels, and Lenin, interpretations of the meanings of those teachings have differed through the years. The basic psychological postulates of Marxist theory—consciousness as the product of social factors in the environment, a materialist approach to studying phenomena, the rejection of self-interest as a major motivation, the superiority of the collective over the individual, the supremacy of rationalism, and an emphasis on rewarding social relations as the means to self-actualization—have remained fairly intact. Western personality theory is still seen, for the most part, as subject to the jaundiced view of human nature put forth by the capitalist philosophers.

While Marx's views about human nature were limited to the theoretical, Soviet psychologists have faced the difficult task of putting these ideas into practice. In so doing, they have developed a system with some new features that distinguish it from both orthodox Marxist formulations and Western psychology as well.

After an initial flirtation with psychoanalysis in the 1920s, Soviet psychologists came to regard Freudian theory and its derivatives with contempt. The emphasis on sex, individualism, irrationality, psychological rather than historical determinism, and the pessimistic outlook that characterizes psychoanalysis are antithetical to Marxist theory. The Freudian emphasis on the loneliness of the individual and the basic misery of life did not fit well with a psychological theory holding that the essence of man lies in social relations.

Freud's emphasis on the unconscious also presented a problem

for the Marxist psychologists. If men are motivated by unconscious
wishes and needs, then they are not responsible for what they do.
While the unconscious may be a useful construct when dealing with the
mentally ill, it plays a relatively small part in the lives of normal individuals. In the Soviet view, man is a conscious, rational being who
is able to appraise a situation accurately and take purposeful action.
He is not a slave to repressed infantile desires and rages.

The question of responsibility had been a preoccupation of Soviet
psychology since the 1920s, and resolution of this problem led to the
disenchantment with American behaviorism mentioned earlier. The
initial enthusiasm for behaviorism and its emphasis on environment
and training waned as Soviet psychologists found the theory unable to
account for individual responsibility. If consciousness and character
are solely products of environmental factors, then how can maladaptive
behavior arise in an ostensibly conflict-free socialist society?

Under the Criminal Code of 1919, children of 14 were not considered responsible for criminal activity since such activity was considered to be a result of the unhealthy environment of prerevolutionary
years. As the Soviet Union moved closer toward its goal of achieving
the healthy environment of socialism, however, children increasingly
came to be viewed as responsible for their actions. In the 1929 revi-
sion of the Criminal Code, children under 16 were eligible for reha-
bilitation, while those over 16 were to be treated as adults. Finally,
in the decree "Concerning Measures for Combatting Crime Among
Minors" in 1935, all children over the age of 12 were to be considered
responsible for their actions. These shifts in the responsibility for
criminal activity from society to the individual coincide with the
achievement of socialism as decreed by Stalin in 1936.

With the new emphasis on individual responsibility after 1936,
training became a critical area of study for the Soviet psychologist.
The Pedological Perversions Act criticized psychologists for taking
on the dubious role of "expert" when it was the teacher in the classroom who was actually doing the job of creating the new Soviet citizen.
Makarenko's book about his experiences in shaping the characters of
allegedly hopeless antisocial youth, The Road to Life: An Epic of Education (1933-35), was enormously popular with the Soviet government
and the public as well. Using a style that was accessible to parents
and laypersons, Makarenko wrote over 200 books and articles about
raising children.

In an application to the Central Institute of Organizers of Peoples' Education to attend a training course in 1922, Makarenko spelled
out his beliefs about the education of children. He argued that children
should never be considered outside their collective environments—that
their relationships with teachers, parents, and other children are extremely important in development. Since school is one of the major

agents for teaching children social values, it should be considered as a system, with the focus of education going far beyond the improvement of teaching methods. The proper education of the child requires a unity of mental, physical, and aesthetic training (Makarenko's schools always had a band), and constructive labor through the collective as an important means of developing character.

More important than the school, however, is the family life of the child. No educational program can overcome problems if the relationship between the child and parents lacks warmth or respect, and the Soviet system, with its paid leave for maternity and breaks for visiting children in nurseries has attempted to reconcile the importance of this relationship with the needs of modern industrial society. Makarenko clearly felt that it was the duty of the teacher to intervene in the lives of children and although cooperation between parents and the school is emphasized, the school tends to have the last word since it controls social mobility. Makarenko felt that reliance upon academic psychological theory was a poor substitute for experience, and he took an active role in banning the use of psychological tests in education in 1936.

In the years since 1936, three-factor theory has given way to four-factor theory. The personality of the individual is now seen as being the product of biological inheritance (the least important factor), environment (which is believed to be capable of fostering a high degree of development in itself), training, and what is referred to as "self-training." The concept of self-training puts particular emphasis on the responsibility of the individual to fulfill his obligations to the collective and to the state. In his observation of child-rearing practices in the Soviet Union, Bronfenbrenner comments on a movement among Soviet educators to develop "individual potentialities" and a shift away from total dependence on the collective.

The exigencies of rebuilding a society after years of czarist oppression led the socialist theorists to some rethinking of Marx's views on human nature. These new ideas have been more on the order of clarifications rather than modifications, however. Except for a few forays into the nonmaterialistic, the Soviet view of personality remains basically congruent with the assumptions of Marxist theory.

Whether or not the Soviets have succeeded in developing a new kind of human, however, is a different question. Soviet authorities, including Yuri Andropov, admit that the construction of the new Soviet man is incomplete, and that it will remain so until a truly communistic society is established. Nevertheless, they also assert, the Soviet Union has made substantial progress toward creating the kind of individual who will constitute the coming communist society—the kind of individual that is the true reflection of human nature.

According to the Programme of the 22nd Congress of the Communist Party, the moral code of the builder of communism includes the following:

> devotion to the communist cause; love of the socialist motherland and of the other socialist countries;
>
> conscientious labour for the good of society—he who does not work, neither shall he eat;
>
> concern on the party of everyone for the preservation and growth of public wealth;
>
> a high sense of public duty; intolerance of actions harmful to the public interest;
>
> collectivism and comradely mutual assistance; one for all and all for one;
>
> humane relations and mutual respect between individuals—man is to man a friend, comrade, and brother;
>
> honesty and truthfulness, moral purity, modesty, and unpretentiousness in social and private life;
>
> mutual respect in the family, and concern for the upbringing of children;
>
> an uncompromising attitude to injustice, parasitism, dishonesty, careerism and money-grubbing;
>
> friendship and brotherhood among all peoples of the U.S.S.R.; intolerance of national and racial hatred;
>
> an uncompromising attitude to the enemies of communism, peace and the freedom of nations;
>
> fraternal solidarity with the working people of all countries, and with all peoples.

9

Beyond Marx and Freud: Reich and Veblen

> My medical experiences with men and women of
> various classes, races, nations, religious beliefs,
> etc., taught me that "fascism" is only the orga-
> nized political expression of the structure of the
> average man's character, a structure that is con-
> fined neither to certain races or nations nor to
> certain parties, but is general and international.
> Viewed with respect to man's character, "fascism"
> is the basic emotional attitude of the suppressed
> man of our authoritarian machine civilization and
> its mechanistic-mystical conception of life.
>
> Wilhelm Reich

WILHELM REICH

In spite of the apparent contradictions between Marxist and
psychoanalytic ideas about human nature, some psychologists have
attempted to create theories that incorporate the best of both schools
of thought. Given the almost mystical attraction of both systems
(analysands are as likely to become proselytes as Marxists), it is
not surprising that some individuals have built careers around bringing these two schools of thought together. The combination of Freud's
insights into human character and behavior and Marx's insights into
the functioning of the economic system and its impact on individuals
seems to offer the possibility of developing a world view that could
explain both human nature and society.

Attempts at syntheses such as these can be risky, however:

Wilhelm Reich was thrown out of the International Psychoanalytic Society for his communist beliefs and out of the German Communist Party for his belief in psychoanalysis. Reich was an extremely controversial individual whose early works on the relationship between body and character led to the mystical science of orgone, the hypothesized life energy that lies within each person. Reich's life ended in disgrace—his ideas about orgone had been totally rejected by the scientific community and he died in the Lewisburg Federal Penetentiary after ignoring a court order to stop selling "orgone accumulators." But he still has many followers today, and his attempt to synthesize Marxism and psychoanalysis led to an intriguing theory with a number of interesting ideas about human nature.

Reich was one of the several of Freud's pupils who quarreled with the master. In 1922 he helped to found the Vienna Seminar for Psychoanalytic Therapy, and he became known as a particularly brilliant therapist who specialized in cases that were difficult to treat. Although in 1908 Freud had introduced the notion of "character structure"—the recognition that certain traits seem likely to occur together in the same individual—it was Reich who fully developed this idea. While Freud's major focus was on isolated symptoms, Reich took an interest in the individual's "style" of functioning.

Reich believed that there were three layers of personality in each individual. At the bottom, most inaccessible layer, people are naturally loving, sociable, and productive. These qualities do not fit in well with the economic structure of a competitive society, however, so the social structure forces the individual to repress them. The result of that repression is the kind of personality that Freud thought was most basic: the neurotic individual motivated by greed, lust, violence, and other unsavory qualities. However, the smooth functioning of society makes the expression of these unsavory qualities unacceptable as well, so the individual develops a "character armor"—a certain kind of deadness and rigidity—that allows him to function effectively in the world. This character armor can be seen in the person's manner of speech, his attitude toward life and other people, his body motions and facial expressions. Reich believed that people developed rigid characters in order to survive the repressive nature of society.

Character armor, however, comes at a rather high price. The more rigid an individual's character, the less his capacity for what Reich called "orgastic potency." Reich came to believe that the basic instinct of life was the discharge of tension through orgasm and that satisfactory orgasms are essential for psychological health. He defined orgastic potency as

the capacity for complete surrender to the voluntary convulsion of the organism and complete discharge of the

excitation at the acme of the genital embrace. It is
always lacking in neurotic individuals.

Reich felt that the exigencies of life, both in childhood and in the
present, make necessary the development of character armor, which
in turn severely hampers the ability of the individual to experience full
and satisfactory orgasms. The ability to experience such orgasms
leads to the expression of the deepest and most positive layer of human nature. Although all orgasms relieve some tension, true orgastic
potency is limited to heterosexual sex without irrelevant fantasies or
unusual practices. Reich felt that orgastic impotency was to blame for
most of human unhappiness, and that the Freudian death instinct was
not really an instinct, but simply the result of unsatisfactory orgasm.

In spite of their differences, Reich always believed that Freud
was sympathetic to his view of the development of neurosis, but that
he had to reject the orgasm theory for three reasons. First, Reich,
himself a Jew, felt that Freud had not sufficiently freed himself from
the sexual rigidity and belief in monogamy that are part of Judaism.
Second, Freud's own unhappy marriage made the recognition of the
importance of orgastic satisfaction too threatening on a personal level.
And finally, Reich felt Freud was probably too old and had worked too
hard to gain acceptance for psychoanalysis to risk his reputation on
sexual radicalism.

Sex and the Social Order

Reich was originally a social democrat who believed that improvement in the lives of workers would come through better knowledge about sexual matters. During the period 1927-30, he founded six
"sex-hygiene" clinics in Vienna for the purpose of providing information about sexuality to members of the lower classes. Although these
clinics were originally supported by the Austrian Social Democratic
Party, they were sufficiently controversial that the party closed them
in 1930. Outraged at the closing of the clinics, Reich came to believe
that the leadership of the Social Democrats was more interested in
furthering their own positions within the established social order than
doing anything to improve the lives of workers. In 1930, Reich moved
to Berlin, joined the Communist Party, and began to establish sex-
hygiene clinics under their auspices.

Witnessing events in Berlin during the 1930s, Reich wrestled
with the question of why the oppressed classes failed to rebel against
their oppressors and why they so often acted against their own interests. In The Mass Psychology of Fascism (1933), Reich argued that
class ideologies become embedded in character. Because most chil-

dren are born into societies that repress sexuality, parents teach their children that the practice of repression is the proper way to function. But the end result of the repression of sexuality is the denial of the positive qualities of human nature.

Echoing Engels, Reich believed that patriarchy is an unnatural state of affairs. Matriarchy is natural to human beings, and in a matriarchal society, there is no domination or repression, no state and no classes. People live in harmony and satisfaction, and there is no need to create the submissive kind of character. Only when the father comes to dominate the family does sexual and class repression begin. For this reason, Reich believed that Marx and Engels were incorrect in asserting that economic redistribution will allow people to return to their pristine state. What both capitalist and socialist workers really need is not economic revolution, but sexual revolution.

The Mass Psychology of Fascism was the immediate cause of Reich's expulsion from the German Communist Party. Reich had written that the character armor necessary to survive in the Soviet Union under Stalin made Soviet communism as repressive an ideology as capitalism. Although Reich felt Lenin and the Bolsheviks had been sincere in their attempt to end patriarchy through legislation passed in 1917, they had been totally naive about the psychological consequences of their actions.

Throughout the 1920s, Bolshevik theorists engaged in a full-scale evaluation of matters relating to sexuality. According to many of the Bolsheviks, the family, whose existence was simply a vestige of exploitative economic relationships, was finished. In its wake, the revolution left many devotees of "free love" as well as widespread promiscuity. "The cult of virginity" was seen as a vestige of the dark ages.

Lenin, however, was known to have felt that the libertinism of the postrevolutionary period had gotten out of hand. Clara Zetkin reported Lenin's feelings on this topic in her book, Reminiscences of Lenin:

> Although I am nothing but a gloomy ascetic, the so-called "new sexual life" of the youth often seems to me purely an extension of bourgeois brothels. That has nothing whatever to do with freedom of love as we Communists understand it. . . . In my opinion the present widespread hypertrophy in sexual matters does not give joy and force to life, but it takes away. . . . The revolution demands concentration. Dissoluteness in sexual life is a phenomenon of decay.

Additionally, Lenin stated, a communist must be "neither monk nor Don Juan."

In 1922, the Bolsheviks established a policy toward prostitution designed to reeducate prostitutes and to punish their exploiters. Prostitutes were required to enter specially established prophylacteriums for medical treatment, education, and training, and between 1926 and 1935, the Moscow prophylacterium treated 3,810 former prostitutes. By 1935, the prophylacteriums were disbanded since prostitution had virtually disappeared from Soviet society, and continues to be very rare even today. In 1927, a decree announced that individuals with gonorrhea who did not seek treatment would be liable to six month jail sentences.

Toward the end of the 1920s, Reich felt, the Soviet leadership had more or less stifled the sexual experimentation of the revolutionary period, and by 1930, Soviet society had essentially reverted to the czarist conceptions about the sanctity of the family and the father's power. To Reich, this was proof that passing laws about economic redistribution cannot solve the basic problems of human life.

In The Sexual Revolution, which first appeared in 1936, the same year as Stalin's decrees about the sanctity of chastity and the dangers of immorality from the dissolution of marriage, Reich analyzed the failure of the Soviet Marxists to create the kind of society that Marx had envisioned. In their naivete with regard to psychology, the Bolsheviks had assumed that the passage of laws that affirmed equality between the sexes would be sufficient to create a new kind of order. In fact, equality constituted such a disruption to the culture that no one could foresee the kind of society that would emerge.

Reich believed that, however well-intentioned the Bolsheviks had been, they were still the products of their own character armor. As divorce, abortion, homosexuality, and nonmale domination of families became more prevalent in Soviet society, both the leaders and the people became increasingly threatened by their own sexuality. One does not remove a submissive character through legislation, Reich argued, and the people were unprepared to deal with the emerging change of values. Given Stalin's high degree of personal character armor, it was unlikely that any attempt would be made to enlighten the people as to the kind of society that true liberation would bring. Fearing the establishment of a society without sexual repression, Stalin and the Soviet people reverted to the fascism that is the natural product of character armor.

In the years since 1936, Soviet society has become, by Western standards, somewhat puritanical. In an interesting study conducted after the Nazis had captured the cities of Rostov and Novorossiisk, all unmarried women in both cities were examined for virginity, and the Nazis found that 85 percent had not engaged in premarital intercourse. The first kiss shown in a Soviet film did not appear until 1956 and apparently caused something of a sensation. In 1959, during his visit to California, Premier Khrushchev was greatly offended by the cancan girls who danced for him as entertainment.

As in most modern industrial societies, sexual mores in the Soviet Union have tended to loosen somewhat in recent years. In a survey reported by Boris Kerblay, 50 percent of a group of happily married Soviet women saw nothing wrong with extramarital sex. The rate of illegitimate birth in 1970 was 9.5 percent, compared with 23 percent in Sweden and 8.1 percent in the United States. Kerblay additionally reports that the number of unmarried cohabitants in the Soviet Union is quite large, perhaps reflecting a new concern for career in the females, much as their counterparts in capitalist society.

The attitude of the Soviet government toward sexual matters seems to remain puritanical, however. Prostitution is still regarded as a serious crime, with individuals found guilty subject to five years' imprisonment followed by exile. In spite of the large number of publications available to Soviet citizens (who, before they have children, spend an average of 4.35 hours reading per week), these publications contain little that Western readers, accustomed to titillation in novels, magazines, and on television, would find particularly interesting. As David and Vera Mace observed:

> Only those who live for a time on the other side of the Iron
> Curtain, and then return, realize what an enormous part
> sexual stimulation plays in the West in entertainment, in
> advertising, and in social life. In the Soviet Union all this
> is totally absent.

The Natural State of Fascism

Reich came to believe that all persons—capitalist, socialist, or otherwise—are fascists under the social facade that they present to the world. As their parents raise them to fit into repressive societies, children develop rigid identifications with whatever social order they are born into. The leadership of all societies will do everything they can to make certain that sexual rigidity, which ensures the fascistic character of individuals, is maintained. Sexual freedom threatens the established order, and hence must be extinguished. An example of this might be seen in the United States, where some homosexual groups have maintained that the government is thwarting research into acquired immune deficiency syndrome (AIDS) as a means of eliminating homosexuality.

Yet the rigidity of the character armor is seen not only in deviant groups, but in all people. Character armor is not merely psychological, taking its form in reactionary political views, but is also evidenced in the manner in which people carry themselves and their alienation from their bodies. In Reich's view, numbers of sexual partners and varieties of positions have nothing to do with psychological health. The most obvious indicator of the rigidity of most humans is their poor quality of orgasm. Character armor precludes the fullest release of tension that comes through true orgastic potency. Reich believed that only through the fullest expression of orgasm can human nature be truly expressed.

Like Freud, Reich was a deviant whose ideas did not fit in well with either the capitalist or socialist societies of his day. It is clear, however, that his version of the future is much more in line with Marx's ideas than with those of Adam Smith. Reich was always an opponent of the conservative nature of capitalist society with its purported exploitation of the worker and the resulting alienation. He agreed that the pristine state of human affairs had been overthrown with the rise of capitalism, but he felt Marx had fallen short of recognizing the means of recapturing that state. Whereas economic redistribution is one step in rectifying the perversion of human nature that occurs in capitalism, it is not enough. The character armor of the communist makes him just as susceptible to fascism as the capitalist. Reich eventually came to believe that, with regard to character armor, there were no differences between capitalists and proletarians. Without sexual revolution, it makes no difference who is on top.

In 1939, the same year that Reich moved to the United States, he came to believe that the world was suffused with a kind of life energy called orgone. The remaining years of his life were devoted to the study of orgone and to increasing conflicts with the scientific community and the Food and Drug Administration, who believed his orgone accumulators were fraudulent. While still adhering to the goals of Marxism and Marx's belief in the natural good of man, Reich had moved to the more radical position of believing that the free flow of orgone energy throughout the universe was the key to allowing men to manifest their natural selves.

Reich felt that his ideas had always been too radical for any authorities—capitalist or socialist—to tolerate. In his will, he stipulated that his papers be sealed for 50 years after his death, hoping that a new generation would not be afraid of his ideas. The book he was working on at the time of his death in 1957 was lost, presumably destroyed by prison officials.

THORSTEIN VEBLEN

The quest for profits leads to a predatory national policy. The resulting large fortunes call for a massive government apparatus to secure the accumulations, on the one

hand, and for large and conspicuous opportunities to
spend the resulting income, on the other hand; which
means a militant, coercive home administration and
something in the way of an imperial court life—a
dynastic fountain of honor and a courtly bureau of
ceremonial amenities. Such an ideal is not simply a
moralist's day-dream; it is a sound business proposition.
(Thorstein Veblen to President Theodore Roosevelt)

Thorstein Veblen (1857-1929) was an economist and social critic
whose ideas about human nature are not widely appreciated by many
economists and are virtually unknown to psychologists. Yet Veblen's
insights into the manner in which economic culture shapes personality
and human behavior often seem particularly appropriate for describing
life in modern American consumer society. Although not to the degree
of Reich, Veblen himself was a controversial figure who was known
for his philandering, quarrels with authority, and utterly cynical view
of Western culture. As historian Henry F. May commented: "In Veblen's description of society, and also in his curious career with its
spoiled jobs and broken marriages, there seems to be a tendency to
equate whatever is pleasant, luxurious, or conventional with evil."
Like several other theorists discussed in this book, Veblen had no
intention of creating a theory of personality, but his comments on the
effects of economics on the individual, and particularly his ideas about
human instinct through the ages, have a kind of implicit theory of personality behind them.

Although Veblen greatly respected Marxism, believing that there
was "no system of economic theory more logical than that of Marx,"
he also felt that Marx and Engels had let idealism color their views
of human nature. Whereas Marx had seen class conflict resulting in
the inevitable demise of capitalism and its replacement with a humanitarian socialism, Veblen drew upon anthropology, sociology, history,
and perhaps behaviorist psychology to argue that such a result is far
from inevitable. In actual fact, Veblen asserted, history shows that
workers don't want economic redistribution, meaningful work, or rewarding social relations. Workers will always choose material goods
over self-actualization or social relations. The desire for Model Ts,
Victrolas, and sliced bread is a far more powerful motivation than
any wish for social justice.

Veblenian Civilization

Like Marx, Veblen believed that mankind had originally had a
kind of idyllic existence. During the savage era, which Veblen believed

was the most protracted period in human history, people lived peacefully, had little property, no class distinctions, and a minimum of authority relations. Again as Marx, Veblen believed that this period was characterized by female dominance. But in contrast to Marx, Veblen did not believe that this state of affairs is natural to man. History, in the Veblenian view, is subject to progress and regress, and the time of peacefulness is probably irretrievable.

As technology improved, survival became less of an issue for mankind, and the age of barbarism began. The human struggle against the environment became the struggle against other humans. During this phase, class structures, bellicosity, private ownership, and patriarchy became established. Veblen saw this period of human history lasting until the close of the Middle Ages.

At the end of the Middle Ages came the handicraft era, which is the origin of modern civilization. During this period, the major reward of work was the job itself, not the wages that come from doing the work. However, the quest for efficiency put an end to the handicraft era. In the ensuing modern era, the business interests of the middle class eventually become the dominant cultural value. Class differences slowly dissipate, and a precarious peace, necessary for the maintenance of the economic system, is established.

Human history is also characterized by the rise of what Veblen referred to as "pecuniary emulation." Pecuniary emulation refers to the tendency of humans to compare themselves to others and to desire the things that others have. This instinct of comparing one's state to others is the driving force in American consumerism. As a rule, people determine what things they feel they must acquire by looking at the possessions of the class above them. A contemporary example is the modern fascination with the name of a "designer" attached to clothing, telephones, or automobile interiors. Because the designer's name is inscribed on the object, there is a feeling of exclusivity. This attitude of pecuniary emulation is one of the most observable qualities of American civilization, where gourmet popping corn, greeting cards for mothers-in-law, dog foods that promote longevity, and other creations of Madison Avenue serve to provide Americans with new items to consume.

It is a major thesis of this book that individuals who are able to appreciate the value of consumption have a natural advantage in adapting to American culture, and those who do not understand American consumer society will have a harder time. When I asked one refugee why he left Cuba, for example, he told me it was because conditions were so terrible that there were no shirts to buy. In contrast, former Soviet psychiatrist Edgar Goldstein has likened the experience of the Soviet immigrant entering the United States to that of neurotics entering psychotherapy:

And in fact, many immigrants, when asked the question,
"Why did you leave Russia?" answered "Because I wanted
to breathe freely." This is the same phrase that some
native American neurotics use when asked why they came
for treatment.

In Veblen's framework, the Cuban who held the pecuniary value
of wanting to buy shirts will have a much easier time adapting than the
Soviets who wanted to breathe freely.

Veblenian Instincts

Like many others, Veblen was greatly influenced by Darwin in
his view of human nature, and he felt that men must be considered as
animals that are driven by certain basic instincts. Among the constructive instincts are the parental bent, which is the instinct to provide for future generations; the instinct of workmanship, which leads
humans to seek quality, efficiency, and enjoyment in production; and
the instinct of idle curiosity, which has resulted in learning and science.

On the other hand, men also carry within them the destructive
factors. Echoing the capitalist philosophers, Veblen believed that men
have an instinct for individual enterprise, which leads to predatory
practices toward other individuals and toward society. Men also have
an instinct to establish institutions that utilize "force and fraud" to
carry out their objectives. Finally, men have an instinct of exploitation or sportsmanship which is a holdover from prehistoric hunting
societies. Organized athletics, where one wastes effort and skill in
nonproductive activity, is the paramount example of this instinct.

Veblen believed these instincts were found in all people, regardless of class, but that they appear in different strengths in different
periods. The instinct of workmanship and the parental bent were strong
in the savage period, but waned at the coming of barbarism. As part
of Veblen's view that history is progress and regress, they reemerged
during the handicraft era, but the demands for efficiency which gave
rise to the modern period led to the contamination of the instinct of
workmanship. Whereas production was once controlled by individuals
who enjoyed what they were doing, efficiency has required that control
now be vested in accountants, CEOs, and shareholders far removed
from the actual production. One of the most objectionable qualities of
capitalism is that it has kept the constructive instincts subordinate to
the destructive.

In a society where pecuniary emulation is the driving force,
workers are willing to sacrifice their own interests in their pursuit

of the goods that the leisure class holds. Mankind does not necessarily act on the basis of rational decisions, but, Veblen argued in a manner similar to the behaviorists, are more susceptible to habit or convenience. As such, individuals are likely to participate in actions that are contrary to their own interests. For example, Veblen's comments about the kind of person people choose for leaders:

> A degree of arrested spiritual and mental development is, in practical effect, no bar against entrance into public office. Indeed, a degree of puerile exuberance coupled with a certain truculent temper and boyish cunning is likely to command something of a popular admiration and affection, which is likely to have a certain selective effect in the democratic choice of officials.

Veblen and Marx

In The Theory of Business Enterprise (1904), Veblen's discussion of the effects of industrial capitalism seems prescient of the state of capitalism in the 1980s. Veblen suggested that as industry continued to grow, power would become increasingly concentrated in the hands of a few. This concentration would lead to an excess of production which leads to pervasive recessions. Pervasive recessions naturally give rise to labor unrest. In order to deal with labor unrest, patriotism and militarism become paramount values in the society. Finally, labor is kept under control and the recession is relieved by the absorption by the military of excess production.

This is an extremely wasteful system, Veblen argued, but it is the natural culmination of diverting human needs into emulation of the leisure class. Although Veblen's critique was directed at the capitalist system, this analysis also seems appropriate for the Soviet Union in the 1980s, where socialist zeal replaces the acquisition of consumer goods at the level of the workers, but where leaders such as Brezhnev were able to collect sports cars and dachas as a hobby.

Veblen was in accord with Marx in seeing the interests of the workers and the leisure classes as being in inevitable conflict. Veblen had an extremely cynical view of modern business practice, which he saw as being motivated solely by greed and without consideration for the common interest. In contrast to his contemporary, Calvin Coolidge, consider Veblen's views on advertising:

> [Advertising] is a trading on that range of human infirmities which blossom in deviant observances and bear fruit in psychopathic wards.

Similarly,

> the arts of business are arts of bargaining, effrontery,
> make-believe, and are directed to the gain of the busi-
> nessman at the cost of the community, at large and in
> detail.

Unlike Marx, Veblen was not optimistic about returning to the human nature of the days of primitive communism. He seemed to feel that modern industrial practice precluded opportunities for human nature from the time of savagery to blossom. Whereas Adam Smith may have been relevant for understanding human nature in a society characterized by small merchants, the idea of competition improving personality was no longer useful in the complex business world of the twentieth century. Veblen used the example of the formation of U.S. Steel in 1901 to demonstrate that theories about man as independent operator had become irrelevant. U.S. Steel had been formed from 11 corporations that owned a total of 785 operating plants. When capital becomes that concentrated and competition consequently becomes nonexistent, then Smith's ideas about the independent operator as representative of human nature are of little value.

Veblen also thought the capitalist philosophers, and Bentham in particular, were incorrect in simplifying human motivation into the mere pursuit of pleasure. In The Place of Science in Modern Civilization (1919), he wrote:

> The hedonistic conception of man is that of a lightning rod
> calculator of pleasures and pains, who oscillates like a
> homogeneous globule of desire of happiness under the im-
> pulse of stimuli that shift him about the area, but leave
> him intact. He has neither antecedent nor consequent. He
> is an isolated, definitive human datum.

Veblen felt that this was a misunderstanding of human nature since the pursuit of pecuniary emulation, which governs so much of our lives, is clearly an irrational process. Additionally, Veblen agreed with Marx that human personality is not static, but a product of relations to both the environment and to the individuals within it. Because the industrial world has grown so complex, however, there is little hope for quality human relations on an individual basis. For life to be tolerable in the future and for the business culture to continue to exist, wrote Veblen, totalitarianism will probably be necessary.

Like Reich, Veblen was interested in the question of why the oppressed classes fail to revolt against their masters. Instead of repressed sexuality that leads to fascism, Veblen felt that the drive of the lower classes toward emulation of the upper was the major force that kept the social order. As long as the lower classes believe that they have a chance of winning the Publishers Clearing House Sweepstakes or acquiring a Gold American Express Card, then there is virtually no chance for revolution.

Since Veblen considered revolutionary zeal to be naivete in the extreme, he tended to take the pragmatic view. He felt that the system of capitalist business enterprise was so strong that the Bolshevik Revolution would be overthrown. The only way for the Bolsheviks to retain power would be through dictatorship, so the people would actually be no better off under communism.

REVISING THE MASTERS

One reason the theories of Reich and Veblen are interesting is because they are both attempts to go beyond the ideas of Marx and Freud and to create new kinds of theories. In a sense, Reich's theories are as utopian as those of Marx; Veblen is as pessimistic about human nature as Freud.

Like Marx, Veblen did not intend to formulate a theory of personality. Nevertheless, his conceptions about the nature of society and the effects of economics on individuals imply a perception of human nature that could be a basis for a personality theory. In spite of Veblen's wide range of interests, it is unlikely that he was familiar with the works of Freud. Given Veblen's appreciation of the strength of habit in behavior, however, it seems quite likely that he was familiar with the works of the early behaviorists. Although it is virtually certain that Veblen would have dismissed stimulus-response theory as being too simplistic, his concept of the lower classes emulating the upper is not unlike the present day behaviorist conception of "modeling," which is discussed in Chapter 12. Whatever his knowledge of psychology, however, Veblen apparently preferred to rely upon sociology, anthropology, history, and economics to formulate his views of human nature.

Reichian theory, on the other hand, has its roots in biology and psychoanalysis. Assuming that satisfactory orgasms are the major motivation in life and the key to both psychological health and a humane society, Reich developed a position that is probably the most radical in this book. Both he and Veblen seemed to accept the hypothesized harmony in personal relationships that was ostensibly found in prehistory as being the natural state of human nature. But while Veblen felt that history had taken man too far to return, Reich believed that the free flow of orgone energy through the body could return man to the rewarding world of prehistory.

Both Reich and Veblen took a negative view of the world as it is. They recognized the inhumanity of the capitalist system and they made suggestions as to how to change it. Whereas Veblen suggested change on the macro-level—social planning or totalitarianism—Reich believed in individual change through better orgasms.

Throughout his life, Reich was continually in conflict with authority. He was evicted or forced to resign from organizations and expelled from countries because of his radical views. Veblen's conflicts with authority—generally with his wives and university administrations—were not so dramatic as those of Reich, but they were just as recurrent. In a sense, both men were iconoclasts who were unable to accept the rules of the societies in which they lived. While both of them condemned the capitalist system, by the end of their lives, Reich and Veblen seemed to have had little hope in the working class. The character armor of fascism and the mindless aping of the leisure class preclude the establishment of rewarding human relations. However noble man's intentions, his willing compliance to the established social order will always make the achievement of meaningful social relations just a dream.

10

The Third Force

Our culture, based increasingly on the conquest
of nature and the control of man, is in decline.
Emerging through the ruins is the new person,
highly aware, self-directing, an explorer of inner,
perhaps more than outer space, scornful of the
conformity of institutions and the dogma of authority. He does not believe in being behaviorally
shaped, or in shaping the behavior of others. He
is most assuredly humanistic rather than technological. In my judgment he has a high probability
of survival.

Carl Rogers

One of the most striking things about refugees who begin the process of adaptation to American culture is the personal tragedies that
almost each has known. Stories of the violence experienced by refugees
are both sickening and amazing. Whatever one may feel about revolutionary change, the fact is undeniable that in the chaos that follows,
many innocent people suffer. Not only are family members likely to
have been arrested, tortured, and killed by the incoming regime, but
those family members who are left are apt to lose their jobs, homes,
and all material possessions. They are also likely to suffer consider-
able humiliation and persecution because of their former roles in the
society or their ostensible connection to people judged to be enemies
of the new regime. Application for permission to exit generally inten-
sifies this persecution.

In many cases, escape means a bribe in gold and a journey by
sea where pirates are a danger and where passing freighters won't

99

necessarily give assistance if your boat is sinking. Overland journeys usually require passing through areas where marauding armies and bandits are equally dangerous. Upon arrival at the destination, refugees are sent to virtual concentration camps (be it in Thailand or Fort Smith, Arkansas), where there is nothing to do but wait for something to happen that will allow for release. Once the refugee has found a sponsor and enters American society, all the things that he or she hasn't had time to think about—specifically the tremendous loss of home and family and the dangers that remain for family members left behind—come back to haunt the refugee. When a student of the school where I worked would receive bad news from Indochina, an almost palpable feeling of sadness would descend upon the entire school. So many people had lost so much that any bad news would bring back memories of what had been experienced.

With that kind of history, these individuals faced the task of learning a new language, new customs, finding a job and a home, and enrolling their children in schools where they would no longer have control of what the child learned. In spite of what appeared to be insurmountable difficulties, the great majority of these people succeeded in making at least a modicum of adaptation to American society. In existentialist terms, the experience of the refugee is testimony to the triumph of the human spirit. When human beings show their ability to rise above the most horrible kinds of conditions and experiences, then ideas of human nature that focus on libidinous drives or stimulus-response theories are just too limited to explain the actual human experience.

The psychoanalytic and behaviorist views of human nature were the reigning personality theories in Western capitalist cultures until the rise of existentialism and humanistic psychology in the 1950s. Humanistic psychology, designed to present an alternative to both psychoanalysis and behaviorism, is part of the "third force." Third force psychologies are defined, above all, by a sense of optimism about human nature and the possibilities for psychological growth.

Although the ego psychologists had replaced Freud's pessimistic view of personality with a more upbeat emphasis on environmental factors, life is still seen as a struggle between mother and child that rarely has a happy ending. Although their environmental emphasis tends to bring psychoanalysis more in line with U.S. capitalist culture, the ego psychologists still focus on the importance of the first years of life and the difficulty of overcoming problems from that period. For this reason, ego psychology remains a pessimistic theory.

In many respects, behaviorism is as pessimistic about human nature as psychoanalysis. According to the behaviorist viewpoint, if people are not taught to be warm, open, life-affirming individuals, they won't naturally be so. They can just as easily be made into unthinking automatons who are able to engage in brutality and destruction without any negative feelings whatsoever. Whereas psychoanalysis is an amorphous, almost mythical theory asserting that guilt and sexual repression is the glue holding civilization together, behaviorism offers a concrete means for side-stepping concepts such as guilt and training individuals to behave in any way their trainers desire. Films such as The Manchurian Candidate and Clockwork Orange have impressed this fact upon millions of Americans.

To many people in the West, the depressing fact about behaviorism is that it holds human nature to be entirely at the mercy of environmental manipulation. All human achievement, from the Bayeux tapestry to the theory of relativity, can be seen as nothing more than responses to environmental stimuli. Behaviorists believe that human behavior, like dog behavior, is simply the product of training, and that concepts such as free will and personal responsibility are myths we use to deny this fact. Such concepts are deleterious, in fact, to the establishment of the well-ordered and efficient world system that will be necessary to meet human needs in the future.

As suggested above, the third force was designed to challenge the overarching pessimism of both psychoanalysis and behaviorism. In recent years, the third force has split into a myriad of factions, practices, and schools of thought, but the unifying factor in all third force psychologies is an emphasis on the strength of the will of man, man's instinctual movement toward psychological growth, and a rejection of either environmental or instinctual determinism. While the philosophical roots of psychoanalysis are traceable to Nietzsche and Schopenhauer, and of behaviorism to the British empiricists and the scientific method, the original philosophy of third force psychology is existentialism—itself an extremely pessimistic philosophy that grew out of a reaction to the popularity of Hegel.

EXISTENTIALIST HUMAN NATURE

In addition to arguing that the contradictions of the world resolve themselves in God, Hegel had suggested that the universal was always superior to the particular, and that the abstract nature of the state was naturally superior to the particulars of any individual's life. In Phenomenology, Hegel had argued that the renunciation of individuality was necessary for the transition to positive freedom—the freedom of living within the state and the society.

At Berlin University in 1841, F. W. Schelling had presented a critique of Hegel's philosophy in a famous series of lectures attended by the anarchist Bakunin, Engels, and Soren Kierkegaard. Kierkegaard, who found Schelling's lectures quite boring ("Schelling drivels on quite intolerably," he wrote), was nevertheless impressed by the Hegelian system. Of particular interest to Kierkegaard was Hegel's denigration of the individual and exaltation of society. After the series of lectures, Kierkegaard returned to Copenhagen and wrote his rebuttal to the Hegelian system, Fear and Trembling (1843), which is regarded as one of the first statements of existentialist philosophy.

Sartre has suggested that although Kierkegaard's work went virtually unnoticed in the nineteenth century—Fear and Trembling was not translated into English until 1933—existentialism reappeared in the twentieth century as a European reaction to the excesses of Soviet Marxism. As Western enthusiasm for Marxism waned in light of Stalinist policies during the 1930s, individuals were looking for a philosophy of action that was keeping with the spirit of Marxism that they felt the Soviet Union had lost. Existentialism, whose relationship to Marxism Sartre himself described as "a parasitic system which lives on the margins of the real science," seemed to offer a means for regrouping the frustrated socialists of Europe and the United States.

After World War II, existentialism became popular in the United States, influencing all the social sciences, and psychology in particular. Eschewing both the Marxist and the pessimistic elements of existentialism, American proponents and the humanistic psychologists that followed them repackaged the system in order to make it more congruent with the belief system of American capitalist culture. Although the world view of Kierkegaardian and Sartrean existentialism in no way offers an optimistic view of man and his place in society, American psychologists developed existentialism into the most optimistic of all views of human nature.

In contrast to Freudian free association and Watsonian experimentalism, existentialists gather data for their position through an approach called "phenomenology". Phenomenology requires transcending all preconceptions, philosophies, or prejudices and trying to look at the phenomena of this world as they really are. Reliance upon explanations such as laissez faire, dialectical materialism, Oedipal victor, stimulus generalization, or other such terms is not allowed in the existentialist framework. To be intellectually honest, people must step outside such dogmatic explanations for phenomena. Given the strength of the preconceptions that all people hold, however, man is able to transcend his prejudices, existentialists argue, only through the most rigorous and careful kind of rational thinking. Insofar as it is possible, men must avoid being caught in the consciousness of their societies and the people around them.

At this point existentialism deviates a great deal from Marxist theory, and this deviation has led to the rejection of existentialism by those holding to the Moscow line. Marx and Engels wrote that consciousness is a product of the historical conditions in which man finds himself, and so there is no reason to assume that the ways in which men see the world do not change over time. While men are rational, that rationality is still always a product of specific periods in history. The phenomenological approach suggests that man can remove himself from his historical context to understand the events of the world. This belief that man can somehow step outside the dialectic of history is not acceptable to Soviet Marxists.

According to the existentialists, man sees two depressing facts when he looks at the world rationally. First, he sees that he is truly, irrevocably alone. He sees that the ultimate fact of life is that he must die, and that he will do so alone. No amount of positive social relations can alter this fact.

Second, a rational approach to understanding the world reveals that life on this planet is a horrifying nightmare of death and destruction. The history of the human race is one of almost unmitigated tragedy, and people who believe otherwise are self-deceived. Such phenomena as wars, genocide, refugee experiences, and the basic anxiety that comes with living in the twentieth century make the contributions of so-called scientific and technological progress seem almost negligible. In the face of powerful forces such as Peacekeeper missiles, cluster bombs, SS-20s, television, Gosplan, drug traffickers, the KGB, and Political Action Committees, people feel helpless and alienated—that what they do won't make any difference any more.

When men see the world as it really is, they are morally compelled to do something about the nature of life on this planet. In this respect, existentialism borrows from Marxism the concept of praxis: the idea that individuals cannot be satisfied with mere philosophizing, but must act to apply their philosophies to the matters of everyday life. Whether or not their actions make a difference is not so important to the existentialists as the fact that they are obligated to do something about the sufferings of humanity. The world is such a depressing place that the chance of any individual making a substantial contribution to the lessening of others' suffering is slight, but each individual is morally bound to try.

Phenomenology and rational thought have given man the terrible burdens of both recognizing the tragedy of life and requiring him to act even when action may be futile. In another sense, however, they give man reason for hope. Man realizes that the human spirit is more powerful than anything in the world, and through this spirit man can individually transcend the sufferings of this world.

Further, by freeing himself of the illusory baggage of ideology, man is free to search for a personal meaning in his life. This search for meaning is not prompted by sexual drives or even the pursuit of happiness—it is rather an attempt to avoid the anxiety of living in a world so filled with tragedy. If man sees the tragic nature of the world, he has the choice of dishonestly deceiving himself and denying the misery—which is in fact what most people do—or he can attempt to do something about that misery. The importance of rational choice is the quality of existentialism on which third force or humanistic psychology focuses.

HUMANISTIC PSYCHOLOGY

Humanistic psychology has taken a number of existentialist beliefs and put them into a framework that eschews the pessimistic and emphasizes the positive values of human existence. Humanistic psychology concurs with existentialism that the individual is personally responsible for his existence and that the human spirit can transcend the tragedies of this life. The individual is far more important than any collective, and because the way in which each individual sees the world is unique, theories, dogmas, and ideologies that are applied to everyone are oppressive. The most important factor in the life of any individual is not his essence—the state of his birth—but his experience. Individuals born in the worst of circumstances, such as Abraham Lincoln, for example, can rise to high positions, and it is this belief in the inherent potential for individual growth and improvement that makes humanistic psychology and popularized offshoots such as _est_ and other growth ideologies so attractive to members of capitalist culture.

Humanistic psychology holds an extremely positive view of human nature. Unlike the Freudian view that each person is a seething cauldron of destruction, or the behaviorist view that people are anything that they are taught to be, humanistic psychologists hold that people are naturally good. Individuals are seen as being intrinsically creative, open to new experiences, and always looking for opportunities to optimize their potentials through self-growth. Rather than seeing the purpose of life as holding down the instincts or having no purpose at all except to respond to stimuli, humanistic psychology stresses the inherent movement toward self-improvement that is allegedly found in all human beings.

Humanistic psychologists maintain that this drive for self-improvement is genetic but that its unfolding is greatly influenced by the environment, much as Marx felt that the species-being of man was also influenced by the environment. Humanistic psychologists such as Carl Rogers would agree with Marx that most of us never realize a fraction of our potential because of environmental factors. But whereas Marx would attribute this deadening of the individual to economic factors and the competition to survive, Rogers attributes the stunting of individual growth to problems with authority.

According to Rogers, as a child interacts with the environment—

and this usually means the psychological, rather than the physical, environment—he forms a self-concept about who is he and what he can do. Some of the values that constitute the self-concept of the child are from experience, but many of them come from other people. In fact, the major problem of modern life is that there is always someone around telling us who we are and how we should act. We learn to believe that what people tell us, rather than our own experiences, is true, and we try to meet their expectations of us rather than be who we really are.

However, these beliefs told to us by our parents or teachers or spouses are usually not based on experience, but rather on their own belief systems, probably handed down to them by their own parents or teachers. Rules as to what constitutes "good" behavior and "bad" behavior are crammed into the child's head to such a degree that eventually the child loses touch with his "self"—that part of his personality that knows naturally what is good and bad. Eventually the child has virtually no autonomy and must always rely upon a set of rules in order to know what to be.

Humanistic psychologists believe that, deep inside, people are basically good and, if left to their own devices, they will inherently know what is good for themselves and act accordingly. We must always be on guard against people who tell us who we are and what we should be doing, just as we must guard against government interference in the natural economic order. These people who tell us what to do may or may not know what they are talking about, but the sad fact of modern life is that most of us end up denying what we know intrinsically to be right and adopting the viewpoints of others instead.

Rogers called the state of relating that fosters the optimal psychological growth "unconditional positive regard," which occurs when individuals are accepted for what they are and no one tries to foist his opinions on them. If individuals are given unconditional positive regard, they will feel psychologically secure and able to extend positive regard to others.

According to Rogers, the natural state of man leaves him open to experience, he has an organismic trust in himself and his decisions, and he does not need the judgment of others. Man is a free agent who will take responsibility for his actions, and he is always creatively seeking new experiences. The belief systems of Adam Smith and Carl Rogers are congruent in holding that the essence of man does not lie in social relations, but within the self-interest of the individual.

Self-Actualization

Humanistic psychologists are obsessed with a concept of growth known as "self-actualization," a term that is used by many of the theo-

rists in this book. Self-actualization, the drive toward which humanistic theorists believe to be genetic, occurs when an individual consistently moves toward an optimal state of existence characterized by
self-improvement, happiness, and satisfaction. Since the best Freud
could offer was changing "neurotic misery into common, ordinary unhappiness," or Watson maximally adaptive responses to stimuli, then
it is not surprising that many Americans have so enthusiastically em-
braced self-actualization psychology.

As the chief proponent of humanistic self-actualization theory,
Abraham Maslow offered a theory of personality based upon a hierarchy of needs that he felt was genetically based. Individuals need, first
of all, those phenomena that are necessary for survival. When those
needs are met, individuals then require that their world be secure,
consistent, and orderly. When individuals feel secure, their next need
will be for affectionate and intimate relationships (which, Maslow has
commented, are almost impossible to fulfill in modern America). When
individuals are loved, then they will have self-esteem and the need to
be recognized and appreciated. Finally, when all four previous layers
of needs have been met, an individual will experience the need for self-
actualization—the desire to fulfill one's highest potential.

What are the characteristics of the self-actualized person?
First, he or she has a special kind of awareness of self, nature, and
the world. The self-actualized person will not be fooled by the dogmas
of politics or religion and will have a more democratic character
structure. Emotional life is enriched and spontaneity is enhanced.

The self-actualized know their feelings and they trust them.
They feel a bond with the entire human race and are free of prejudice.
They react to people as individuals and not on the basis of race, creed,
color, or role that the individual happens to be playing. According to
Maslow, self-actualized people are truly free—they are independent,
creative, and private. They accept themselves and they accept others
without necessarily adopting their values. Their own values come from
within. Self-actualized people are not perfect, but they seem to be
functioning at a higher level and reaching a potential that most others
cannot seem to grasp.

HUMANISTIC PSYCHOLOGY AND CAPITALIST PERSONALITY

As might be deduced from the foregoing, humanistic psychologists tend to have a world view that is virtually congruent with that of
Adam Smith. Humanistic psychologies all emphasize the importance
of the individual over social relations or the collective. Whereas most
humanistic psychologists express some concern about the quality of
human relations, it is obvious that their first interest is the psychology

of the individual. Like Adam Smith, they adhere to the notion that progress must come on an individual basis first and benefit to society will follow. The historical conditions in which one is born are not nearly so important as an individual's desire to succeed or improve himself. Further, the individual is seen as somehow knowing within himself, independent of the teachings of culture or the people around him, what is best for himself, and by extension, what is good for society. He will maximize his own human potential and, consequently, everyone will benefit.

Second, humanistic psychologists believe in the melioristic view of life. Since humans have a genetically endowed tendency toward growth, the full flowering of human nature is something that is achievable. The major hindrance to this flowering, however, is the authorities who subvert the truths that we hold within us. Humanistic psychology takes a dim view of anything that is imposed from above. Truth comes from within and must be experienced—it cannot simply be told to us.

Humanistic psychologists believe that an individual can rise above the environment in which he finds himself. Factors such as social class, heredity, home environment, quality of family life, culture, religion, and past experience can be overcome. Humanistic psychologists tend to regard these factors with suspicion—rather than giving us identities, they keep us from discovering our real selves. While they may have an effect on who we are, we are not bound by them and we can always rise above them. Humanistic psychology rejects categorically the dialectical view about the inevitability of class conflict.

Like the capitalist theorists, all humanistic psychologies take an extreme view of freedom, holding that the ultimate source of authority resides within the individual. Man must be free to do absolutely anything he desires. Because of their inherent goodness, however, self-actualized individuals will not engage in any practices that harm other people. By developing their own potential to the fullest, those around self-actualized persons will benefit. It is an often-noted paradox, however, that people come to humanistic therapies because they feel alienated from others and from themselves, only to have the therapist encourage them to get more in touch with their "real selves," rather than society's values, becoming in the process even more individualistic and alienated.

AMERICAN POP PSYCHOLOGIES

In both the Soviet Union and the United States, the desire for self-improvement seems to be strong. In the Soviet Union, where consumer goods are not widely available, both status and upward mobility tend to be based on acquiring an education. Soviet citizens spend a surprising amount of time studying while they are working. Overall, 20 percent of Soviet men and 15-17 percent of Soviet women devote some time each week to studying.

In the United States, on the other hand, there exists what Erich Fromm has called a "personality market"—a variety of psychotherapies and experiences to help individuals get more in touch with their real "selves." Some of these experiences include Gestalt therapy, Arica, Scientology, polarity therapy, transactional analysis, rebirthing, est, and many more. Although many of these self-actualization programs have been dismissed as being self-enrichment schemes for their originators, many do offer fragments of humanistic personality theories that reflect the values of American capitalist culture.

est is a down-to-earth psychology that focuses on the achievement and experiencing of the "self" within the framework of one's everyday activities. The est self is transpersonal—"beyond any individual, identification, form, process, or position." As in Rogerian psychology, the est self represents what we truly are—our true human nature stripped of commitments, belief systems, traditions, etc. Culture, religion, social class, and other role determinants are seen as neurotic baggage that we cling to for definition and that keeps us from experiencing our real selves.

In the est system, most individuals are seen as existing in a state called "Mind" rather than "Self." Mind is a storehouse of memories that individuals use for survival. But more than mere physical survival, individuals use memories for ego protection as well. In every case where the person has felt threatened—and particularly in the childhood years—the mind has recorded the experience. When a person feels threatened anew, the mind will replay the experience even if it is not at all related to present circumstances. The individual will then respond as he did to the original threatening experience, no matter how dissimilar the two situations. That is to say that the actions of adult individuals are very often responses to threatening situations of early childhood, in spite of the fact that there are no connections between the two experiences. est postulates, therefore, that the responses of most people to most situations are inappropriate.

The basic conflict within individuals, according to est founder Werner Erhard, is survival or perpetuation of "positionality," i.e., holding to a belief about something, vs. wholeness or self-actualization. People who are stuck in Mind are stuck in the past and consequently perpetuate grievances from long ago. They also cling to anything that gives them an identity. One gets free of Mind and experiences Self by participating in a 60-hour training program held during two successive weekends.

est training seeks to create an "econiche" for the "transformation" of the individual—a catharsis of problems from the past and an experiencing of the true Self. Once the true Self is experienced, est holds that an individual will be free to develop his potential. The implicit personality theory of est is much like self-actualization theory: individuals are intrinsically good but are somehow corrupted by society. Returning to this state of pureness can only be beneficial. est holds that transformed individuals will create transformed relationships and transformed environments. Like the capitalist formula holding that the improvement of one leads to the improvement of all, transformed environments will lead to the positive functioning of institutions and a better life for everyone.

est and many of the self-improvement programs have been widely accepted within the capitalist cultures of the United States and the West. Many have been phenomenally successful business enterprises and have attracted thousands of converts willing to participate in programs that can be quite costly. Their originators have clearly identified a need people want to have filled.

In spite of their popularity, however, most of these programs offer no unique ideas about human nature. Borrowing from psychoanalysis, behaviorism, humanistic psychology, Eastern mysticism, and science fiction, they have repackaged specific concepts into human development programs that are a confirmation of the values of capitalist culture. They subscribe to all the capitalist values—the importance of self over society, individual responsibility, a meliorist view of the individual and the world, the pernicious effect of government, rational thought, and the unlimited potential of every human being regardless of his situation. Rather than being outside the culture in which they are practiced, self-improvement courses tend to teach their adherents that the values of capitalist culture are psychological and transcendental truths that lead to happiness. The ultimate goal of these ideologies seems to be an enlightened conformity.

HUMANISTIC VERSUS HUMANITARIAN

On the whole, psychologies of the third force have fragmented in recent years into such a diversity of approaches—including such schools as Tibetan Buddhism, extraterrestrial psychology, megavitamin theories, and others—that it is difficult to predict the future direction of humanistic psychology. A willingness on the part of many humanistic psychologists to include all sorts of deviant schools under their umbrella has given humanistic theories a bad name with many academic psychologists. Joseph Rychlak, himself a humanistic psychologist, suggests that the present dissaray in humanistic psychology is the result of a confusion between the terms "humanistic" and "humanitarian." While megavitamins may share with humanistic psychology an emphasis on the human, rather than instinctual or environmental, aspects of personality, megavitamins are for improving, but not necessarily understanding, human nature.

Whatever the case, in spite of a strong initial showing, third force psychology has apparently failed in its attempt to dislodge psychoanalytic and behaviorist approaches from their regnant positions in Western personality theory. In recent years, an additional challenge to the self-actualization movement has come from psychologists such as Robert Hogan, who use sociobiology and evolutionary theory in their approaches to personality theory. Sociobiologists in particular criticize humanistic theories on the basis that since animals have no biological imperative to self-actualize, why should self-actualization be accepted as a genetic drive in humans?

In evaluating third force psychologies, the resemblance between the personality theories and the assumptions of capitalist culture is striking. Individuals need to substitute a belief in Self for belief in tradition or culture. The third force Self, with its extreme emphasis on individuality, however, is clearly congruent with a capitalist, rather than socialist, culture. So in spite of all the rhetoric about self-actualization, third force psychologies end up confirming the dominant capitalist cultural values. The end to alienation apparently comes through a reconversion to the capitalist system.

11

Socialist Humanism

The central question of socialism remains the
elimination of the problem of man's alienation in
modern society, and not merely the attainment of
the Western level of consumer goods. Socialism
is not primarily about forms of ownership, but
about the measure of human freedom. We do not
have to be ashamed that we have only half the
national income of the Western countries, but
should be ashamed that we possess less than half
their civil rights.

Ivan Svitak, Prague, 1968

Although Marx was concerned about aspects of human nature
such as alienation and the depersonalization of the individual, his
major focus was usually the workings of the capitalist economic system. Marx wrote less and less about personal happiness, human essence, or alienation after the Economic and Philosophical Manuscripts
of 1844. After 1844, the emphasis of Marx's works shifted to the social
plane—the nature of society as a whole, rather than the nature of the
individuals who constitute that society.

The socialist philosopher Adam Schaff has suggested that this
change in emphasis was the result of two historical factors. First,
Marx and Engels came to recognize that the redistribution of wealth
would come only through revolutionary struggle and not through philosophical argument, and hence they redirected their activities toward
the polemical, rather than the philosophical or psychological. Second,
Marx and Engels also recognized the need to cooperate with lesser

theoreticians who were not as interested in developing ideas about human nature as much as they were in overthrowing governments and redistributing wealth.

This difference in emphasis in the writings of the so-called "early Marx" and the "mature Marx" has led to some polemics in Marxist circles. Whereas one group of socialist scholars and practitioners suggests that the early Marx is the "true" Marx and that the state of modern socialism is the result of regrettable historical developments, other Marxists have maintained that the concern for the humanity of the individual in the early works is only youthful idealism rather than well-developed philosophy and political theory. Not surprisingly, the official ideology of the Soviet Union subscribes to the latter idea: the early works of Marx are not important for understanding socialism, but are useful in understanding the evolution of Marx's thought. The early works have been quite influential, however, in Marxist circles outside the Soviet Union, particularly since the 1960s and especially in Yugoslavia.

Socialist humanists believe that the failure of the Soviet Union to live up to the humanistic elements of Marxist theory, the perversion of communism in service of Soviet nationalism, and the use of Marxist theory only so far as it justifies Soviet ideology, have actually alienated the Soviet Union from the most basic teachings of Marx. Yugoslavian socialists further believe that if the teachings of Marx had been followed, Stalin could never have survived in the Soviet Union. Whereas the Soviet Union was founded in the hope of creating—or, more aptly, recreating—a kind of self-actualized individual, Stalin finished all possibility of achieving this dream. Even after his death, Stalin's followers continue to sacrifice Marxism for Soviet statist and imperialist ambitions. The purge of first the Left Opposition, then the Right Opposition, the massacre of the Kulaks, the Nazi-Soviet Pact, Yalta, Czechoslovakia, Afghanistan, and Soviet complicity in banning the Solidarity movement in Poland are ample evidence for the socialist humanists that the Soviet Union has lost the thread of Marx's understanding of human nature.

The realization that a Marxist state could be as oppressive, exploitative, and dehumanizing as a capitalist state, writes the Yugoslavian socialist humanist, L. Marković, occurred to members of the worldwide socialist movement too late:

> They overlooked only one thing: that in certain historical
> conditions the victorious workers' vanguard may alienate
> itself from the rest of the class, seize all the levers of
> economic and political power, and establish its own sec-
> tioned rule. The socialist revolutionaries became con-
> scious of this nightmare only when it already became true.

HUMANIST REVISIONISM

The traditional model of Marxism, writes Adam Schaff, is inadequate because of its lack of focus on the problems of the individual. Individual problems remain a critical issue even within the collective. The revolutionary seizure of the means of production may lead to more equality in economic distribution, but this will not necessarily make people happier or closer to their true nature. Millions of people live under socialism, yet psychologically, they appear to be no better off than exploited Western workers who must look to consumerism for satisfaction in life. In fact, the misery of alienation is shared by workers in both systems.

Nevertheless, the problem of the individual remains a problem of social relations. It is the striking failure of most modern socialist governments to concentrate on the human relations aspect of Marxism, argue the socialist humanists, that causes the socialist worker to be just as miserable as the capitalist worker. Just because a socialist government runs the industrial sector and ostensibly shares the wealth with the worker, the quality of human relations, contrary to what Marx predicted, does not seem naturally to improve. People still do not have that unique spirit of cooperation and personal satisfaction that allegedly characterized life before the rise of industrial civilization. As evidenced by the Soviet experience, simply ending the domination of capital over the life of the worker does not automatically restore meaningful human relations.

Marković has written that Marx's concept of the "genuinely human society" includes the high development of productive forces, an abundance of material goods, and an existence mostly free of imposed labor. Echoing Veblen, production becomes a process where the individual "objectifies his potential sensual and intellectual powers, affirms his personality and satisfies the needs of other individuals." In Marković's life-affirming society, there are no money, markets, ideologies, religions, divisions of labor, or professional politicians.

Socialist humanists are united in believing that their thinking represents Marx's ideas about human nature more accurately than the socialist theorists who concentrate upon the redistribution of wealth. Sixty years of socialist control of the means of production in the Soviet Union has failed to produce a higher quality of social relations. For this reason, the focus of the socialist humanists is on the individual and his social relations first and the economic structure second.

THE YUGOSLAV EXPERIENCE

For socialist humanism, the major strategy for restoring the depth of human relations lost from early times is through democracy and freedom—and certainly not the pale imitation of what passes for freedom in Western societies. Human relations obviously cannot reach the pristine state of earlier days without the establishment of the kind of democratic society where all men are valued and each is free to develop his species-being. Such a democracy cannot occur when a government, socialist or otherwise, is pursuing policies to keep itself in power. Individuals will never be able to express their true nature, will never be free, they and their work will never be valued, and the quality of their relationships with other humans will remain unsatisfactory so long as they don't have control of their lives. So far, write the Yugoslav humanists, only the Yugoslavian system has made any attempt to allow for this democracy.

In 1942, as Tito and the communist partisans were fighting to liberate Yugoslavia from Nazi control, Stalin cut off aid from the Soviet Union. In Stalin's view, the Yugoslav resistance movement had shown too much independence from Moscow policies. During the war and until Stalin's death in 1953, Yugoslav leaders struggled to develop their own kind of socialism, which they felt would be more in keeping with the model that Marx had in mind in the Economic and Philosophical Manuscripts. The Yugoslavs felt that the goals of revolutionary Marxism had been sacrificed for bureaucracy in the Soviet Union, and that the Soviet Union was no longer fit to be the leader of the world socialist camp. In defiance of Stalin, the Yugoslavs demanded equality among the communist parties of all countries, equality among all socialist governments, and the right of each socialist state to independent action.

In contrast to the Soviet system, the Yugoslavs moved to decentralize their economy in 1949. In place of centralized planning, most industrial decisions were to be made by the Worker-Management Councils that today are found in almost every organization. In large organizations members are elected to the councils, whereas in organizations with less than 30 employees, everyone is a member. Members serve for two-year terms at no extra pay, and they remain responsible for fulfilling the duties of their regular positions during their time on the council. The councils approve management decisions, appoint management personnel, set salary scales, hire and fire, and do long-term planning for the organization.

In a further move toward decentralization, party meetings were opened to nonmembers, and agricultural collectivization was abandoned in 1953. In their program of 1958, the Yugoslav Communist Party declared that the personal happiness of man cannot be subordinated to

higher goals, since personal happiness is the highest goal of socialism. Additionally, individuals should have the right to express opinions and religious feelings, as well as "the inviolability and integrity
of human dignity, and his personality." Marxism is not a dogmatic
and rigidified theory, the program stated, but in accordance with the
Hegelian dialectic, is open to change and reinterpretation.

The Soviet Communist Party, which regarded the Yugoslavs as
revisionists, boycotted the meeting at which the 1958 program was
introduced.

ERICH FROMM

The basic contribution of the socialist humanists to understanding human nature thus far has been their focus on the importance of
the individual in socialist society. Although they have introduced a
important critique of the orthodox Marxist understanding of human
nature—economic redistribution alone does not lead to personal ful-
fillment—socialist humanists generally rely upon Marx's ideas for
their own conceptions about human nature. Erich Fromm was clearly
the most psychologically-minded of the socialist humanists. Trained
in psychoanalysis in Munich and at the Berlin Institute during the 1920s,
Fromm devoted much of his life to forging a synthesis between psychoanalysis and Marxism. Along with Adorno, Horkheimer, and Marcuse,
he was a member of the Frankfurt School of critical theory and was
displaced to the United States in the 1930s.

The Frankfurt School had been founded in 1923 around the study
of philosophy, social analysis, and the Left Hegelians of the 1840s.
Members of the Frankfurt group were critical of capitalism and of
socialism as it was being practiced in the Soviet Union. They emphasized the libertarianism of Marx in contrast to Stalinist practice, and,
like Veblen, they criticized capitalism on the grounds that it subverts
all nonacquisitive values. In the capitalist system, men are worth only
what they can earn, and being free in capitalist society means being
free to choose what goods to consume. Consumption is not an adequate
sublimation for meaningful social relations, however, and people in
capitalist society are basically lonely. As Marcuse suggested, "The
antennae on every house, the transistor on every beach . . . are as
many cries of desperation—not be left alone. . . . "

Like Maslow, Fromm believed that there are basic needs that
humans strive to fulfill: relatedness, transcendence, rootedness, identity, and frame of reference. The need of relatedness requires that
people must be able to relate to others and to experience love. According to Fromm, this ability to relate to others is not something with
which the individual is born but must be learned. This contrasts with
Marx's position that relatedness is a natural function of man.

Second, in accord with Marx, Fromm believed that people must experience transcendence by becoming creative. They need to be able to act upon their environments and change them. Although this is a creative function, the neurotic individual, in contrast, changes the environment through destructiveness. Third, individuals must have the feeling of rootedness: they need to feel that they belong and that they have something in common with other human beings.

All individuals must develop a sense of identity. Failure to recognize one's unique qualities leads to mindless conformity. Finally, people need a frame of orientation and devotion. That is to say, people need an ideology or belief system by which they can make sense of the world. It is not important that the belief system be correct, but rather that the individual can use it to make sense of what is happening to him. In Fromm's system, society was created in order for man to fulfill these five needs. Although Fromm considered himself a Marxist, it is interesting to note that he tended to hold to the misanthropic view of human nature that prevails in psychoanalysis. People are not naturally cooperative, but must learn to be so.

The Marketing Personality

Fromm believed that individuals develop one of seven different types of character. The receptive character, which is somewhat analogous to Freud's oral type, believes that all good things exist outside oneself. These people love food and drink, are dependent on authority, and are known for their optimism, friendliness, and warmth. They are not reflective at all and tend to be indiscriminate in their choices. According to Fromm, this type is found in cultures where one group has the right to exploit another, and it is not generally found in Americans. The exploitative character also sees all good things as outside oneself, but uses force or cunning to achieve his ends. Others are judged by their usefulness, and the exploitative character is suspicious, cynical, and jealous. This type of orientation is common in laissez faire capitalists.

The hoarding character, which is somewhat like Freud's anal type, believes that security comes from saving. He is miserly in money, feelings, and thoughts. This type is noted for his cleanliness and punctuality, and his highest values are order and security. The hoarding orientation was widespread in the eighteenth and nineteenth centuries during the rise of capitalism, and is typified by the Puritans.

Fromm's fourth type, the marketing character, is the most modern type and is most frequently found in Western capitalist society. This type only became dominant with the rise of the principles of marketing. With this orientation, the self is seen as a commodity and society promotes a veritable "personality market" where one can take self-improvement courses such as est in order to be able to "market" oneself more effectively. The primary values of the marketing character are adaptability, ambition, and sensitivity to the expectations of others. The marketing personality strives to be attractive, to dress stylishly, and to exhibit personality characteristics and behaviors that appeal to others. The marketing personality practices exhibiting sincerity, friendliness, and warmth appropriate to situations, and identity becomes "the sum total of roles one can play." The only permanent quality of the marketing orientation is its malleability.

Fromm is not clear where one finds the fifth type, the productive character. This character is free and independent, is guided by reason, and experiences himself as the measure of his productiveness. This individual seems to be a refinement of Marx's ideas about the essence of human relations. Fromm's description of the ideal society wherein this type would exist—which he calls "Humanistic Communitarian Socialism"—sounds like the world the socialist humanists believe Marx envisioned after the seizure of the means of production.

Although Fromm introduced his character types in 1947, he added two new types in his book, The Anatomy of Human Destructiveness, in 1973. These are the necrophilous and the biophilous characters, which Fromm admitted are influenced by Freud's concepts of life and death instincts. The necrophilous character, as described earlier, is obsessed with death and destruction. Unfortunately, for mankind, this type is naturally attracted to political office, and Fromm considered Stalin to be a prototypical necrophilous character. The biophilous character, in contrast, has a passionate love of life and all that is alive. He prefers the new rather than the old, the whole rather than the parts, and attempts to bring about change through love, reason, and example rather than force. Although Fromm is far less specific about the qualities of the biophilous character than he is about the necrophilous, he gives the example of Albert Schweitzer as the prototypical biophilic character.

It is interesting to note that Reich, who had discussed his views on society with Fromm in Berlin in the 1930s, felt that Fromm had improperly used some of his ideas. Except for the omission of the orgasm theory, Fromm's views on the natural state of man and the desirable society are actually quite similar to Reich's. Whatever the case, Fromm never cited Reich in any of his works. Fromm did acknowledge his intellectual debt to Freud, however, but he always considered himself a socialist first and a psychoanalyst second. In his comparison of the two systems, Beyond the Chains of Illusion (1962), Fromm describes Freud as merely a reformer, while Marx was the true revolutionary. Probably the most important area of congruence between Marxism and Fromm's version of human nature is the way in which the character types are products of the social system—as opposed to libidinous drives—in which they are found. The marketing character is a twentieth-century American phenomenon that has arisen in response to the needs of the culture.

Yet, as Fromm was fond of saying, "Man is not a blank sheet of paper wherein culture writes its text." The needs for happiness, belonging, love, and freedom are inherent. These needs may be subverted, however, through a process Fromm calls "the social filter," which consists of language, logic, and, most importantly, social taboos. In other words, Fromm's ideas are consistent with the basic idea behind this book: that regardless of basic instincts, the structure of any society will attempt to make certain that people fit into the prevailing system.

SELF-ACTUALIZATION IN THE SOVIET UNION

The Marxist concept of human happiness has been a goal that has thus far eluded individuals raised in socialist states. To theorists such as Marcuse, Marx's idyll of freedom is an unachievable goal:

> The early Marxian example of free individuals alternating
> between hunting, fishing, criticizing, and so on had a
> joking-ironical sound from the beginning, indicative of
> the impossibility of anticipating the ways in which liber-
> ated human beings would use their freedom.

In the Soviet Union at least, one is expected to find happiness and meaning in life by sacrificing for the welfare of society. This route to personal satisfaction is typified by the Stakhanovite movement of the 1930s. During the night shift of August 30-31, 1935, a coal miner by the name of Aleksei Stakhanov started a movement of self-sacrifice for the fatherland by mining 102 tons of goal—14 times the quota—in one shift. The Stakhanovite movement that followed called upon workers throughout the Soviet Union to make superhuman efforts to master techniques that would raise industrial production. In November of 1935, the first All-Union Meeting of Stakhanovites was held in the Kremlin. During World War II, the Stakhanovites initiated the movement of the "200 percenters" (200 per cent of the quota per shift) and the "1,000 percenters" (1,000 per cent of the quota).

Party members were encouraged to become Stakhanovites and to set a standard for other employees. Stakhanovites were written about in newspapers, given the best rations, received preferences in apartment allocations, and were provided with free tickets to movies and theaters. Additionally, they were exceedingly unpopular with other workers, who resented their privileges and felt threatened by the Stakhanovites' increasing quotas without asking for corresponding salary increases.

According to Marx, the most important influence on personality is experience in the work place, and life can only be meaningful if workers have control of the work environment. One of the first goals of the Bolsheviks was to give workers control over industry, and on November 27, 1917, worker control was proclaimed for all industries with more than five employees.

In the Soviet Union, where the majority of enterprises have less than 200 employees, the criterion for success is not profits, but production. Goals for each industry are set by the state planning organization, Gosplan, in consultation with industry. Labor in the Soviet Union is not controlled, and workers are free to choose the jobs they want. Because the Soviet Constitution guarantees every citizen a job, industries must compete with each other in attracting the best workers. Turnover in the Soviet Union is about 20 percent annually, and much higher in occupations where the work is routine. In the light bulb industry, for example, the entire work force turns over every three years.

In the work place, supervisors hold weekly meetings with employees where production goals and performances are discussed. Workers are encouraged to participate politically and to work overtime, and evaluation tends to be in terms of activism as well as production. Bonuses are not handled on an individual basis, but depend upon group performance, and punishments are arranged for "parasites." In sharp contrast to the U.S. system, Soviet managers are responsible for the housing and welfare of their workers, as well as production. At the uppermost reaches of industry, however, success is usually dependent upon personal performance, where executives are rewarded when their subordinates surpass production goals.

Overall, the Soviet system is quite different from the Yugoslav. Because production goals are set by the state planning agency, individual workers have little say about Soviet economic production. The control of supplies in the Soviet Union is administered by the central government, and Soviet factories are often idle during the first ten days of the month and frantic during the last ten. Like the infamous Detroit automobile that is made on a Friday or a Monday, Soviet goods made in the last ten days of a month tend to be of poor quality.

In spite of the weekly meetings and the government taking responsibility for worker's housing and welfare, the socialist humanists would argue that the lack of real worker control makes Soviet socialism only a little better than capitalism. Propagandizing loyalty to abstract notions such as socialist revolution is as meaningless as believing that real freedom has something to do with consumer goods.

Socialist humanism in its present state represents a kind of utopianism that, depending upon one's theoretical predilections, may or may not be true to Marx's ideas about human nature, and which has been severely criticized by Soviet theorists. The major contribution of the socialist humanists has not really been a new idea of human nature, but rather a refocusing of Marxism onto the needs of the individual. The Soviets and their followers are missing the essence of Marxism, they argue, by continuing to concentrate on the economic. The essence of Marxism is humanism, and whereas Marx was correct about the nature of personality, it is the Soviet Union as much as the capitalist West that is preventing its fullest expression.

12

Cognitive Economics and the Transforming Experiment

> My associates and I have been trying to under-
> stand the process underlying the categorization of
> people and the uses and abuses of such categori-
> zation. These cognitive economics are a mixed
> blessing. . . . By searching for good fits to our
> categories of general types, we may misjudge—
> and mistreat—people who poorly fit our precon-
> ceptions.

> Walter Mischel

Throughout this book I have argued that everyone has an implicit
theory of personality—i.e., ideas about human nature—that he or she
is constantly applying in order to make sense of the behaviors and
motives of other people. This theory may be formal, such as psychoanalysis, or it may be based on an informal belief system with ideas
such as people are basically good or all men are sinners. Psychologist George Kelly suggested that every human encounter is characterized by each participant trying to figure out the other's thoughts. Kelly
said that man is like a scientist who tries to understand the world
through consistently applying his theories to the people he encounters.
These theories are not necessarily correct, or even conscious, but
they come from our expectations about other people and govern the
way we act and how we expect others to act.

One approach to understanding the phenomenon of behavior being
the result of how we think others see us is a school of thought called
symbolic interactionism. Symbolic interactionism holds that personality is a process that, like the sound of the tree that falls in the forest, exists only when we interact with other people. Outside of inter-

action, personality does not exist. But personality also exists when we are alone, since our behavior consists of responses to a "generalized other"—an internalized standard of what we think others expect of us. Role theory, which is the model used in this book when discussing the acculturation experiences of refugees, is an extension of symbolic interactionism.

To reiterate briefly, role theory postulates that people learn styles of behavior that they apply to different situations as conditions warrant. They try out these different sets of behaviors until they find the general style that gets the desired responses and feels comfortable to them.

People from other cultures don't necessarily know the roles that we find appropriate to life in the United States. For example, two Ethiopian refugees were invited by their sponsors to go to a demonstration against U.S. involvement in El Salvador. The weather was quite warm on the day of the demonstration, but the Ethiopians showed up in army fatigues, black berets, dark glasses, and heavy boots. During the demonstration, the Ethiopians kept sharp lookout for government troops while the American demonstrators, in their T-shirts and cut off jeans, danced to the music of the rock band on the stage. The role of demonstrator is apparently quite different in the United States and Ethiopia, and the refugees had to learn that Americans use demonstrations as opportunities to be outside in the sun as much as to express political opinions.

Symbolic interactionism and role theory per se has never caught on with American psychologists. Given the experimental and behavioral bias that prevails in American psychology, concepts such as "role" and "generalized other" are too ill-defined to be accessible in an experiment. Psychoanalysis has little use for roles, since all that is important in human life occurs intrapsychically, and humanistic psychologists disdain symbolic interaction because acceptance of a role amounts to acceptance of someone else's values and the subversion of both autonomy and responsibility.

Nevertheless, American psychologists over the past decades have been developing a theory of personality that is in some respects similar to the symbolic interactionist position. Specifically, psychologists have utilized the social learning theory of Albert Bandura in conjunction with the personal constructs theory of George Kelly to explain the behavior of individuals in terms of the way that they perceive their environments. This approach to understanding personality is called cognitive social learning. Cognitive social learning theory is presently the dominant force in U.S. academic personality theory.

SOCIAL LEARNING AND PERSONAL CONSTRUCTS

As suggested earlier, psychologists Albert Bandura and Richard Walters introduced a new approach to the behaviorist view of personality called modeling or observational learning in 1963. In contrast to the classical behaviorist approach, Bandura and Walters developed the argument that a great deal of learning takes place without reinforcement and is accidental, rather than trial and error. In fact, the authors argued, most of what children learn is simply through observing adults and copying their actions.

In contrast to Watsonian or Skinnerian behaviorism, modeling is both a social and a cognitive theory: most of what we learn occurs in social contexts, and our behavior is very much affected by what we think. Whereas Watson believed that thinking was simply the movement of the speech muscles and more or less irrelevant to behavior, Bandura and his associates hold that thinking is the critical factor in determining behavior. Although both Skinner and Bandura argue from clearly behavioristic perspectives, social learning theory allows for a degree of self-control and autonomy that is impossible within the classical behaviorist framework. Skinner and Watson would hold that changing a person's environment is the way to change behavior, but Bandura's modeling theory holds that changing a person's thinking is a more effective way to bring about change.

Earlier I mentioned the studies showing that children can learn violent behavior simply by watching it on television. If people learn simply by observing, however, then why can't they learn to play the violin by attending concerts or to throw touchdown passes by watching football games? According to modeling theory, there are four conditions that are necessary for observational learning to occur. First, the learner must be paying attention to the behavior to be learned. Second, the learner must be able to recall what happened. Third, the learner must have the physical or mental capabilities of performing the behavior being observed. Finally, and perhaps most important from a personality theory point of view, the learner must have the motivation and incentive to perform the behavior. This last point is critical in differentiating social learning theory from classical behaviorism. Social learning theory relies upon the postulation of nonmaterialist, nonobservable qualities that exist somewhere other than in the environment. At this point, Kelly's notion of personal constructs becomes relevant.

George Kelly (1905-67) believed that cognition—what people think, as opposed to instincts or environment—is the most important factor in personality. Through their experiences, people develop templates of ideas through which they view the world. What people think, regardless of the accuracy of their perceptions, will determine what they do. Early childhood experiences or environmental stimuli are not nearly so forceful in determining personality as the set of beliefs about the world that we carry around with us. If an individual has a view of the world that is virtually invulnerable to modification, then the environment in which that person operates will have little effect on behavior. If, for example, an individual believes that the basis for all science is set forth in the first book of the Old Testament, then advances in paleontology, genetic engineering, or astrophysics will have little effect on how that person sees the world. Similarly, if one blames the socialists for the tragedies that has happened in one's life, then the template of socialism will always bring a negative reaction. This was demonstrated by Indochinese students who, when Mitterand was elected president of France in 1981, held an emergency meeting to discuss what the new socialist government might do to their relatives who had emigrated to France.

COGNITIVE SOCIAL LEARNING THEORY

During the late 1960s, social learning theorists criticized traditional personality theory for being too narrowly focused on the person rather than on the environment in which the person operates. The so-called "situationists" argued that most human behavior can be explained by cues in the environment, and that there is little reason to look to the individual for explanation of behavior. Other psychologists held that it is the individual who is the critical factor and that environmental cues play a subordinate role. In true Hegelian fashion, however, the opposing theses of the person/situation debate resolved into the synthetic viewpoint of cognitive social learning theory. The major spokesperson for this view is former situationist Walter Mischel.

According to the cognitive social learning theorists, behavior (which is held to be the same thing as personality by all behavioral theories) is the result of interactions between persons and situations. That is to say, individuals interpret environmental cues through their own cognitive processes and act accordingly. In the cognitive social learning view, the fallacy of personality theory in the past has been its emphasis solely on person factors, as in psychoanalysis or trait theory, or solely on environmental factors, as in classical behaviorism.

The proper task for modern personality theorists, according to psychologist Norman Endler, is "description, classification, and systematic analyses of situations, stimuli, and environments" and the "examination of how persons and situations interact in evoking behavior." All cognitive social learning theorists are in agreement that the proper study of the interaction between the person and the situation is to be undertaken using the experimental method.

Mischel has argued that individuals, and particularly clinical psychologists who should know better, have a tendency to categorize people and make judgments about them simply on the basis of their own prejudices. This process of attribution, according to Mischel, has obscured the proper understanding of human nature. While the individual may in fact be a scientist as George Kelly suggested, the methodology he or she uses is not very good:

> He or she thus takes little account of statistical and ab-
> stract information about what logically ought to be com-
> pelling and relies instead on objectively less reliable but
> subjectively more vivid, concrete, compelling informa-
> tion, rapidly forming general conclusions from a few
> memorable instances of the sort that characterize per-
> sonality descriptions and vignettes. All the statistical
> reports about the good repair records of Volvos, for
> example, may be readily forgotten when one hears about
> a friend's personal traumas with one Volvo clinker.

In other words, man-the-alleged-scientist has a tendency to use what anthropologist A. F. C. Wallace called the "anecdotal veto": most of us judge the world, and especially the behavior of others, through the personal sets of categories and experiences that we have developed, and we tend to overlook or deny evidence that contradicts our theories. The categories we use are usually nothing more than personal beliefs and are often immune to modification. In trying to understand others, we practice what Mischel has called "cognitive economics": "the recognition that people (including scientists) are flooded by information that somehow must be reduced and simplified to allow efficient processing and to avoid an otherwise overwhelming overload."

The problem with role theory or symbolic interactionism, which are also approaches to understanding the behavior of others through one's personal interpretations, is that they accept these broad cate-gorizations and ignore the actual behaviors that fall within a hypothe-sized role. (Additionally, they emphasize social interaction over other environmental stimuli.) When we ignore behavior, we are likely to make misinterpretations. This is most clearly illustrated by attributing national characters to people: describing someone as being "so Ger-man" or "so British" calls to mind a number of stereotypes that may have nothing to do with individual behavior.

If we look at actual behavior, we are likely to find an infinity of differences between Germans, British, socialists, or any other cate-gorization of people. Cognitive social learning theorists suggest that the kind of sloppy generalization that is the backbone of role theory is typical of any personality theory that is not firmly rooted in the experimental analysis of behavior.

Nevertheless, cognitive social learning theorists utilize several concepts that are highly compatible with the jargon of sociological role theory. In cognitive social learning theory, the categories people use to make generalizations are not roles, but "consensual prototypes." Personality is "interaction competencies," which consist of "the ability to adopt the perspective of other actors." Rather than being the product of ideas about a "generalized other," behavior may be the result of a focus on "other person categories."

The most unique point about cognitive social learning theory is its strict reliance on the experimental method in the study of personality. Holding fast to its behaviorist roots, cognitive social learning theory eschews what it calls "mentalism"—the postulation of factors that cannot be studied empirically. Even though cognitive social learning theorists rely upon such seemingly nonmaterialist notions as motivation and cognitive structures, they accept the experimental study of these phenomena under the rubric of "neomentalism." The problem with personality theory in the past has been its very unscientific reliance on mentalistic phenomena. As psychologist A. Paivio has asserted, only the detached neomentalist can approach mentalistic phenomena without being led astray:

> Mentalistic ideas are so seductive that one is in danger
> of being led by them down the garden path of introspec-
> tion and mysticism forever. For that reason, perhaps
> only a tough-minded behaviourist can afford to entertain
> the seductress.

COGNITIVE SOCIAL LEARNING AND EMPIRIO-CRITICISM

Like classical behaviorism, cognitive social learning theory is ostensibly value-free when it comes to assumptions about human nature. People will learn to be competitive if society provides them with competitive models; cooperative if cooperative models are available. Although cognitive social learning theorists take a materialist view, arguing that phenomena such as motivation and incentive are in fact measurable, classical behaviorists have accused the social learning theorists of the same kind of mentalism that characterizes psychoanalysis and the other theories.

Cognitive social learning theory also allows a great deal more freedom of choice than does classical behaviorism. Mischel has stated that his landmark book, Personality and Assessment, was written to defend individuality. By holding that the unique cognitive set of each person determines behavior, cognitive social learning theorists have underlined the importance of the individual over the environment. In spite of the recognition of the importance of interaction, the emphasis on the individual in cognitive social learning theory ("the cult of the individualistic 'I' ", to quote Soviet psychologist V. N. Myasischev) is congruent with the fundamental beliefs of capitalist economic theory and in sharp contradiction to the Marxist view of personality.

In cognitive social learning theory, environmental cues must first be processed through the individual before behavior can occur. Because of this, attempts to control behavior through structuring the environment can only have limited success. People will be able to avoid noxious stimuli in the environment through the proper cognitive structure. This belief is also clearly antithetical to the Marxist position that historical conditions will determine the behavior of individuals. Roles, which arise from the historical context into which a person is born, are clearly more compatible with the Marxist viewpoint.

With regard to the melioristic view of the future that permeates the writings of Skinner and the capitalist theorists, cognitive social learning theorists are much more circumspect. Overall, they have focused their enthusiasm on their method: through the experimental analysis of situations and discrete acts of behavior, psychologists will at last arrive at an understanding of both the broad qualities of human nature and the idiosyncratic qualities of the individual. One problem with theories that lack experimental evidence, cognitive social learning theorists assert, is that they tend to make hypotheses that have no basis in fact. If the death instinct or self-actualization do exist, for example, they should logically be quantifiable and experimentally accessible.

This emphasis on data and methodology, however has led to cognitive social learning theory being criticized for its lack of theory. Whereas cognitive social learning theorists are in agreement about using experiments to study person-situation interactions, they have thus far been frustrated in putting their findings into any kind of a theory. Additionally, defining what constitutes a "situation" has proved to be more difficult than first imagined. As with classical behaviorism, however, this sacrifice of theory for the more pragmatic issue of methodology is analogous to the practices of capitalist enterprise. Probably the strongest criticism of American psychology made by Marxist theorists is that American psychologists generally fail to identify the philosophical assumptions of the research they pursue.

Marxists in general take a dim view of the experimental method, particularly when it is applied outside the natural sciences. The experimental method is, in a sense, atheoretical, seeking first to identify testable hypotheses that can later be assembled into a theory. This incremental approach to knowledge focuses on what Trotsky contemptuously referred to as "the small coin of concrete questions." Additionally, Soviet psychologists reject experiments because of endemic errors of measurement which, according to Soviet psychologist A. A. Smirnov, are not acceptable in the humanistic Soviet society.

Marxist hostility to the empirical method can be traced back to the Hegelian dialectic. If, as Hegel and Marx after him believed, the world is made up of opposites that are constantly resolving into syntheses, then the notion that one can isolate an unchanging, completely definable "fact" is mistaken. Nothing in the world is frozen in isolation, but rather exists as part of a transformation. As Lenin stated:

> Dialectic is the doctrine of the identity of opposites—how they can be and how they become—under which conditions they become identical, transforming one into the other.

For the Marxists—and for others who use nonexperimental methods—the problem of experimentalism is that it seeks to isolate phenomena and to study them outside of their historical contexts. Not only will such isolation create an artificial view of the phenomenon being studied, but the phenomenon will very likely have changed by the time it has been measured. Experimentalism, like capitalism, ignores or subordinates historical factors to the state of a phenomenon when it is being measured. Experimentalism further fails to recognize the often veiled relationships between entities and attempts to stop phenomena in time and say that what is at that moment will always be the case. The dialectic, on the other hand, studies phenomena in transition.

MODERN SOVIET PERSONALITY THEORY

Cognitive social learning theory is particularly harsh in its criticism of another school of American psychology, trait theory. Trait theory, which is most closely identified with Gordon Allport (1897-1967) and R. B. Cattell (1905- ——), holds that there are either hypothetical or actual neurological structures in the brain that constitute "traits." People can be thought of as being made up of traits— "aggressive", "neurotic", or "responsible," for example—and it is these traits that govern behavior. According to trait theory, the proper study of personality is through psychological assessment, most commonly the personality inventory, in which a person is asked to confirm or deny statements about himself and his view of the world (e.g., "I never step on sidewalk cracks when walking down the street." Or, "With things going as they are, I doubt if I'm ever going to amount to much.")

But traits are like roles, cognitive social learning theorists assert, in the way that they assume categories that may or may not exist, and in the way they ascribe a far greater consistency to personality than is apparent when actual behavior is studied. Further, trait theorists look at the world backward: trait theory says that a person will steal because he is dishonest, whereas the reason a person is labeled dishonest is on the basis of his stealing. Also, because people sometimes have beliefs about themselves that are simply not correct (for example, two beliefs that everyone seems to hold in spite of all evidence to the contrary are "I have a sense of humor" and "I have good taste"), the method of trait theory—the self-report questionnaire—is of specious merit in studying personality.

As suggested in Chapter 8, however, the Soviets have little respect for trait theory and personality testing in general. Trait theory is equally guilty of trying to stop personality in time and look at phenomena outside their historical contexts. Soviet psychologist V. A. Krutetski commented:

> The mechanistic approach to man, the subjective nature of the interpretation of the results, the attempt to "study", by means of primitive and standardized techniques, an extremely complex object, quantifying personality traits and manifestations—all these factors, which are organically inherent in tests and questionnaires, have forced Soviet psychologists to reject once and for all this antiscientific method.

Starting from the Hegelian dialectic, Soviet psychologists have evolved a methodology that they feel is more reflective of actual events. The "transforming experiment" seeks to measure a phenomenon several times as it is in the inevitable process of change, and the "natural experiment" is simply the observation and recording of phenomena within their natural settings. Data are then reviewed and conclusions are drawn. These methods—which resemble the examples of bad research methodology cited in American psychology textbooks— are the cornerstones of the Soviet approach to data collection.

Psychiatrist Isidore Ziferstein has suggested, however, that since the 1950s, Soviet psychology has been moving away from its dogmatic ideological reliance on Marx, Makarenko, and Pavlov to explain personality. At the All-Union Symposium on Problems of Personality in 1970, the study of personality was recognized as being interdisciplinary, and that it must be pursued in its psychological, medical, and biological components as well as philosophically.

Further evidence of the broadening of personality theory in the Soviet Union is the 1979 Internal Symposium on the Unconscious sponsored by the Georgian Academy of Sciences. This controversial series of meetings debated the question of whether or not the unconscious exists and if it has any role in the personality development of normal people.

In spite of this evidence of a new interest in Western personality theory, however, Soviet ideas about human nature remain firmly within a Hegelian, Marxist framework, and four-factor theory is still considered the basis for explaining personality development. The goal of psychology remains the development and study of the New Soviet Man, which is not yet complete. In spite of what they consider their progress in this area, Soviet psychologists recognize that developing the New Soviet Man—who, of course, is quite different from capitalist man—will take longer than simply achieving economic and social change. As head of the KGB Yuri Andropov stated in 1977:

> The development of the new man in the socialist countries takes place not in a vacuum but under conditions of an intensifying ideological and political struggle in the international arena. And if we compare the 60 years of the new life with the thousands-year-old tradition of private property, psychology, and morals, we should not be astounded to learn that in our society one can sometimes find people who disagree with the collectivist principles of socialism. But the fact that there are fewer such people we can regard as a tremendous success.

13

Competitors or Comrades?

> In concrete fact, in actual and concrete organiza-
> tion and structure, there is no form of state which
> can be said to be the best: not at least until history
> is ended, and one can survey all its varied forms.
>
> John Dewey

In this book, I have focused on the qualities of personality that
American and Soviet cultures try to instill in their members. I have
not attempted to argue that the Soviet Union or the United States has
a "national character" or that there is a "modal" Soviet or American
personality. Rather, I have taken the position that anthropologist
Philip Bock refers to as "social structure and personality"—the idea
that the structure of society strives to create the personalities of individuals within that society. If the Soviet or American individual in-
corporates the behaviors the culture teaches into his behavior, then
ostensibly he will fit in better and be more successful within the culture.

The qualities that the American capitalist culture seeks to perpetuate include competitiveness, consumerism, and a belief in progress. Pragmatism is valued over ideology, and Americans are expected to have a sense of personal responsibility, achievement, and
independence. Americans are also encouraged to look at the phenomena of life from a commercial perspective.

Soviet culture, on the other hand, teaches the socialist values
of devotion to duty, loyalty to the group rather than individual values,
and a belief in abstract goals such as socialist revolution. Social relations are held to be more important than self-interest, and the self-
interestedness of capitalism makes it an exploitative system. Individ-

duals in the Soviet Union are also taught the infallibility of socialism and of the Soviet government in particular.

Both of these sets of values are taught by the institutions of society from earliest childhood and are believed by psychologists in both countries to be reflective of human nature in its most basic form. It is not difficult, however, to find exceptions to these ideas about human nature. When we look at the situations of minorities within each society, we find that many people are not fitting into the scheme of values that either culture is trying to teach. The 3 to 4 percent of the American work force that is chronically unemployed, for example, seems to belie Adam Smith's perspective that in the capitalist system the benefit of one leads to the benefit of all. Similarly, members of the Soviet intelligentsia who wish to come to the West to participate in consumer activities also seem to have failed to develop the kind of character that their culture most rewards.

As suggested earlier, psychologists in either system have not been very successful at separating their own cultural values from what they believe to be scientific practice. American psychologists cling either to idealism or atheoretical experimentalism to try to explain human nature; Soviet theoreticians, irrespective of evidence, cannot bring themselves to admit that Marx might have been wrong about anything. So while we can look to psychologists for ideas about human nature, we have to keep in mind that these ideas are likely to reflect the beliefs that are compatible with the economic systems of the psychologists' cultures.

Although there may in fact be something called "human nature," it is a difficult entity to identify with any certainty. If we look at human history and the state of the world today, for example, the evidence for man-the-misanthrope seems quite compelling. On the other hand, the anthropological and sociobiological evidence that man has always lived in groups where social relations would have to be a critical factor for survival also seems compelling. At this stage in our knowledge, subscribing to either belief system seems to be largely a matter of personal choice.

Volumes have been written about the issues with which the capitalist and socialist philosophers have wrestled, but if we step outside the theoretical and look at the phenomena of everyday life, there seem to be some general observations about human nature that can be made.

IS MAN RATIONAL ?

Although Soviet and American social scientists may consider themselves rational, it is not difficult to see that most people in any society do not operate with a rational system of thought. Based on his experiences in the 1930s, Wilhelm Reich wrote about his encounter with the irrational side of life. The fact that people will allow themselves and their families to starve in the midst of plenty, to vote for people whose interests are clearly opposite their own, and to die for causes that are ideological rather than material are testimony to the fact that people do not think or behave in a rational manner.

Although the irrationality of individuals is most easily viewed in the political arena—where, for example, calling a nuclear missle a "Peacekeeper" is intended to placate people's fear about nuclear war or promising a spot in heaven motivates parents to send their children to fight for the Ayatollah—the irrationality of life is also clearly demonstrated in the marketplace. In the U.S. marketplace, the toothpaste that gives us sex appeal is clearly more desirable than the one that fights cavities, the ketchup that comes out of the bottle more slowly is better than the faster one, and using the laundry detergent with the ultimate cleaning power gives women a unique satisfaction in life. In the capitalist system, billions of dollars are spent convincing us that these are important issues, worthy of serious consideration.

In the Soviet system, the production of consumer goods has always been sacrificed for the production of armaments and heavy industry that will ostensibly advance the goal of socialist revolution at home and abroad. In fact, it is hard to believe that Soviet citizens care more about political struggles in Ethiopia and Afghanistan than they do about sufficient housing, the supply of plumbing to every home, or the availability of consumer goods. The work place discussions that are held to be evidence of Soviet democracy are no substitute for having real control over what is being produced. Soviet workers sacrifice their own satisfactions for government policies in distant parts of the world.

Whether individuals behave on the basis of unconscious motives as Freud suggested, or on the basis of habit as Veblen, Watson, and Skinner believed, it is quite apparent that people make decisions on bases other than rational thought. As any successful salesperson can testify, people buy on the basis of emotion, not rationality. Although we may like to think of ourselves as rational and discerning human beings, it appears that neither the values of Soviet or American societies allow for a rational approach to life.

IS LIFE GETTING BETTER?

In the United States, admissions to mental hospitals have been steadily declining since the 1950s because of advances in psychopharmacology. Because of new discoveries in medication, thousands of people who would have been forced to live in asylums are now able to live normal and productive lives on their own. In the Soviet Union, which emerged from the feudal period 400 years after the West, all people are guaranteed housing, work, and medical care. These examples suggest that, for most people, life in both societies is getting better in terms of technology and services.

In terms of happiness or personal satisfaction, however, the improving quality of life is less discernible. As Skinner suggested, human emotion has not changed much since the time of the Greeks. Man may walk on the moon, but human emotions and experiences remain the same everywhere. People in every society still get depressed, jealous, angry, and commit murder. Leaders today are as much at the mercy of their personal motives and ambitions as they were at the time of prehistory. We disappoint our families and children and they disappoint us. Life expectancies continue to increase, but old age is still characterized by a steady decline in physical and mental abilities. In spite of advances in medical technology, most of us will experience the deaths of our parents and friends. So it seems that, on a psychological level, life is not much different than it ever has been.

Marx believed that equal ownership of the means of production would produce a kind of cooperation that would lead to happiness for all, and the humanistic psychologists believe that personal happiness becomes possible when all basic needs are met. Although people in the United States or the Soviet Union rarely starve to death, it is difficult to say that they are "happier" than individuals who live in developing societies. In terms of human emotion or feelings, we have no evidence that either equal ownership or belonging to a high-income group leads to satisfaction.

If an individual measures happiness in terms of consumer goods and the advancement of technology, then life is unqualifiedly improving in both the Soviet Union and the United States. If happiness is related to emotion or feelings, then things are not really very different, regardless of the economic system. (If we take a psychoanalytic viewpoint, of course, then happiness is impossible anywhere and becomes an irrelevant issue in life.)

IS FREEDOM THE NATURAL STATE OF MAN?

In the United States there is probably no word so overworked as "freedom." Aside from its ideological usage, "freedom" has been used to promote everything from soft drinks to feminine hygiene products. In the context of humanistic psychology and capitalist theory, this word tends to mean that the individual can choose to be anything he wants, to live however he desires, to associate with whom he likes, to believe whatever he chooses, and to do anything that does not break the law or hurt other people.

This view of freedom, of course, represents a kind of idealism that bears little resemblance to reality in the United States or anywhere else. People have very little choice about most things in their lives, and particularly about the important things. People do not choose their economic system or the way they look at the world—their cultures choose it for them.

In the United States, people have to work in order to live decently; if they want to make money, they have to become doctors and lawyers and not artists or professors. Their choice of leaders is limited to two parties, and most likely they will vote for the candidate who spends the most money. White males run the corporations and the government, and women hold the lower paying positions and continue to do the greater share of the work at home. Economic necessity has denied most women, and certainly most men, the opportunity to stay at home and raise the children. In the United States, the more money you have, the higher your IQ, the better your health, and the better the prospects for your children. The best predictor of how much money we will earn in our lifetimes is how much our fathers earned.

Freedom in the United States does mean, to a great extent and as Milton Friedman suggests, being free to choose consumer goods. The wealth of products available to anyone who has the money to buy makes the United States the envy of people around the world. Lower class people from Vietnam were shocked, for example, when they learned that they could afford to own a car in the United States; in Vietnam such a privilege would have been unthinkable. Within the constraints of our incomes, Americans are free to choose what car to buy, what television programs to watch, whether to start their own businesses, what apartment to rent or house to buy, and how to dispose of their money in general.

The Soviet Constitution of 1936 guaranteed its citizens most of the rights that the U.S. Constitution guarantees, including freedom of speech, religion, assembly, the press, and the right to hold demonstrations. Going somewhat beyond the U.S. Constitution, the Soviet republics are guaranteed the right to secede. Marxist ideologues like to assert that people in the Soviet Union, with their guaranteed jobs, free medical system, and day care centers, are actually freer than they are in the United States. Because of the alleged lack of social stratification in the Soviet Union, people are not condemned to an endless competition based on the amount of money one has, but can develop their abilities and become whatever they like.

Like all societies, the Soviet Union is, of course, stratified. Privileges are not so much a product of the amount of money an individual has, as in the United States, but tend to reflect one's status in the hierarchy. Being a member of the Party and the intelligentsia opens doors to privileges that are not available to the general population.

These people are eligible for paid vacations, special shopping privileges, access to better schools for their children, and other perquisites that give them special advantages over their comrades.

In spite of the constitutional guarantees, however, the Soviet Union is a totalitarian state where there is strict control over what is spoken, written, or read. One of the major contradictions of socialist theory seems to be that the development of institutions to handle centralized planning all too easily become instruments for controlling dissent. Because the state controls the economic system, the Soviet Union has no need for freedom of expression. The economic culture will continue without meaningful input from the masses.

In the United States, the economic system controls the government rather than vice versa. For capitalism to be successful, it is necessary to have a minimum of government control. Just as capitalist theorists fight against government interference into the economic system, they argue against any infringement on individual rights. Environmentalists, for example, may be an annoyance to business enterprise in the capitalist system, but their rights are tolerated so that business can also operate with a minimum of interference. As I suggested earlier, Americans do not have a capitalist system because they believe in freedom. The capitalist system requires that they have such freedoms as speech, assembly, and the right to bear arms.

Like everything else, of course, freedom is a relative term, taking on different meanings in different contexts. To speak in absolutes like either the capitalist or socialist philosophers have done serves ideological purposes that obscures any meaningful discussion of the word. On a practical level, if freedom means having the basic necessities of life, many people in the United States are not "free." If, on the other hand, it means being able to publish whatever one likes, then virtually no one in the Soviet Union is "free." In the United States and the Soviet Union, freedom seems to be what our respective cultures tell us it is.

COMPETITORS OR COMRADES?

Although Adam Smith and the capitalist philosophers have viewed man as basically competitive and the Soviet psychologists have described man as being basically cooperative, these notions are too simple to describe human behavior. When there is a crisis in leadership in the Soviet Union, we would hardly say that the Politburo members jockeying for position are motivated by a sense of comradely feelings for their fellow candidates. Similarly, when a flood strikes a small U.S. town and everyone works together to keep the river from overflowing its banks, it is hard to believe that the motivation for helping is entirely self-interest.

Observers of the Soviet scene such as Urie Bronfenbrenner report that Soviet citizens do seem to be more friendly and sociable than their American counterparts. Refugees from other cultures also report that although Americans are friendly and open on the surface, their deeper feelings are almost always kept hidden. These ways of behaving are lessons that are taught by the culture, however, and to argue that one state is more natural than the other is an interesting exercise, but not particularly relevant to understanding the conduct of society. In order for Soviet society to accomplish its goals, the people need to believe that social relations are the paramount factor in life; for the institutions of American society to accomplish their goals, self-interest has to be encouraged.

In fact, self-interest cannot be served if social relations are not given paramount importance. If a child cannot get along with its siblings or peers, if an individual cannot cooperate with the group, or if people will not limit their self-interest in the service of society, then life will in fact be the war of all against all. The major criticism of Freud's theory of the origins of civilization is that a tribe characterized by so little cooperation could not have survived. However much Western psychologists may choose to stress the independence of man, animal studies suggest that the group must come first. Marx was undoubtedly correct in stating that the essence of life is in social relations, for without social relations there would be no life.

Of course there are many people in both Soviet and American societies who cannot be simply characterized as either competitive or cooperative and who lead rather solitary lives. These individuals are the ascetics and deviants within both societies who refuse to respond to what the culture teaches and who develop their own standards and ways of behaving. People who are truly deviant include unsuccessful artists, skid-row derelicts, psychiatric inpatients, and revolutionaries. They have no investment in their cultures and are willing to undergo intense deprivation in order to maintain their own standards. Resisting culture's lessons requires a high psychic price, and very few individuals are willing to pay it.

Given that there seems to be a genetic propensity for humans to live in groups, then it may be that cooperation is the natural state of human existence. But this is not to say that competition is not also a genetic tendency. Group-living animals cooperate in the interest of the group, but they also compete for food or sex when necessary. Obviously both competitive and cooperative modes are acceptable to large numbers of people and people can adapt to either. We can see both the profound differences in these two ways of relating, as well as the amazing adaptability of humans, in the experiences of people from socialist states who come to live in the capitalist system. Most of these people, particularly if they arrive when they are young, eventually make a successful transition to life in a competitive society.

One thing that we can be certain about is that personality or behavior is always changing as people try to adjust to changing demands. As they meet with new situations, people continually fall back on using the repertoire of roles that served them well in the past. When people are thrown into situations where they don't know how to act, then behavior or personality has to undergo some adjustment.

During the summer of 1980, for example, there was a scandal in San Francisco when it was learned that some Cambodian refugees were catching dogs in Golden Gate Park and bringing them home to cook (an immigrant from Hong Kong once told me that black puppies make the tastiest meals). These particular refugees, who were country people who had come to the United States much later than their more Westernized counterparts, considered Golden Gate Park to be a large forest in the middle of the city, and animals roaming there were considered fair game. Some of the dog-snatching Cambodians were caught and arrested, and the problem was reported in the newspaper. Animal lovers were furious and demanded punishment to the fullest degree the law allowed. All schools and agencies that worked with Indochinese were instructed to discuss with their students that dogs running in the park are not to be caught and eaten and that serious punishment would result from this kind of practice. To my knowledge, as soon as the Cambodians understood this, no more dogs disappeared from Golden Gate Park.

In one sense, both the capitalist and socialist economic cultures set us free by teaching us the rules and giving us a framework within which to live them. It is foolish to expect people who have been taught different to know or understand the rules we have been taught since infancy and which we take for granted. Just as the socialist personality struggles to adapt to a competitive society, the capitalist personality cannot conceive of life in a society where individual achievement or expression is not rewarded. The competitors and comrades who make up the world have very different approaches to life, and these individuals will always strive to perpetuate their own cultures. For after all, it is these cultures that, to a very large extent, give us our personalities.

Notes

page/line

3/1   Erikson, E. 1963. <u>Childhood and society</u>, 2nd ed. New York: Norton, pp. 144–165.

3/30   Bruner, E. M. 1956. Primary group experience and the process of acculturation. <u>American Anthropologist</u> 58: 605–23.

3/40   Observation indicates. Ibid., p. 614.

5/1   Trotsky, L. 1975. <u>My life</u>. Middlesex, Eng.: Penguin, p. 524.

5/22   Ouspensky, P. D. 1971. <u>The fourth way</u>. New York: Vintage, p. 33.

6/32   working Soviet wives. Kerblay, B. 1983. <u>Modern Soviet society</u>. New York: Pantheon, p. 136.

6/35   Working American males. Blumenstein, P. and Schwartz, P. 1983. <u>American couples</u>. New York: William Morrow, p. 146.

6/36   female attorneys in the U.S. Labor Letter, <u>Wall Street Journal</u> November 8, 1983, p. 1.

6/36   Working women in the U.S. Harris, M. 1981. <u>American now</u>. New York: Simon and Schuster, p. 92.

7/6   92 Soviet nationalities. Kerblay, op. cit., p. 39.

7/14   white, male, clean-shaven. Kanter, R. M. 1977. <u>Men and women of the corporation</u>. New York: Basic Books, p. 47.

7/22   bureaucratic kinship system. Moore, W. 1962. <u>The conduct of the corporation</u>. New York: Random House, p. 109.

8/31   Brigham, J. C. 1971. Ethnic stereotypes. <u>Psychological Bulletin</u>, 76: 15–38.

9/24   Lenin's suits. Wolfenstein, E. V. 1967. <u>The revolutionary personality</u>. Princeton, N.J.: Princeton University Press, p. 206.

9/39   social character. Fromm, E. 1962. <u>Beyond the chains of illusion</u>. New York: Simon and Schuster, p. 78.

9/44   Reich, W. 1972. <u>Character analysis</u>. New York: Simon and Schuster, pp. xxii–xxiii.

10/15   White, L. 1975. <u>The concept of cultural systems</u>. New York: Columbia University Press, p. 126.

page/line

10/30   Allport, G. 1961. Pattern and growth in personality.
New York: Holt, Rinehart and Winston, pp. 9ff.

11/12   Katona, G. 1980. Essays on behavioral economics. Ann
Arbor: University of Michigan Press. 1963. Psychological analysis of economic behavior. 1963a.
The relationship between psychology and economics.
Psychology: The study of a science, vol. 6, edited
by Sigmund Koch. New York: McGraw-Hill.

13/1   Marx, K. 1975. Economic and philosophical manuscripts
of 1844. In Early Writings. New York: Vintage, p.
361.

14/29   Harris, M. 1977. Cannibals and Kings. New York: Random
House, pp. 165ff.

14/41   592 per mile. World Almanac, 1983, p. 572.

15/9   Black Death. Harris, Cannibals, p. 172.

15/18   Weber, Max. 1958. The Protestant ethic and the spirit of
capitalism. New York: Charles Scribner's Sons,
1958.

15/38   Calvin. Troeltsch, E. 1950. The economic ethic of Calvinism. In Protestantism and capitalism, edited by
R. W. Green. Lexington, Mass.: D. C. Heath, p. 22.

16/6   Tawney, R. H. 1959. Religion and the rise of capitalism.
In R. W. Green, op. cit., p. 40.

16/9   Robertson, H. M. 1959. A criticism of Max Weber and
his school. In Green, op. cit., p. 80.

17/43   Smith, A. 1937. An inquiry into the nature and causes of
the wealth of nations. New York: Random House,
p. 14.

19/13   self improvement. Ibid., p. 324.

20/4   Mitzman, A. 1973. Sociology and estrangement. New
York: Knopf, p. 135.

21/5   Holland, J. L. 1966. The psychology of vocational choice:
A theory of personality types and model environments. Waltham, Mass.: Blaisdell.

21/17   Holland, J. L. 1979. The Self-Directed Search professional manual. Palo Alto, Calif.: Consulting Psychologists Press, p. 3.

23/1   Hawthorne studies. Roethlisberger, F. J. and Dickson,
W. J. 1939. Management and the worker. New
York: Wiley.

23/11   Socialist critique. Bramel, D. and Friend, R. 1981.
Hawthorne, the myth of the docile workers, and
class bias in psychology. American Psychologist
36: 867-78.

page/line

23/19   communitarianism. Wilson, E. 1940. To the Finland
           station. Garden City, N. Y.: Doubleday.

25/1   Edison. Ginger, R. 1965. Age of excess. New York:
           Macmillan, p. 312.

26/1   Wilhite, V. G. 1958. Founders of American economic
           thought and policy. New York: Bookman Associates,
           p. 123.

26/32   Aryan races. Hofstadter, R. 1955. Social Darwinism in
           American thought. Boston: Beacon Press, p. 48.

26/38   Sumner, W. G. 1963. The absurd effort to make the
           world over. In Social Darwinism. Englewood Cliffs,
           N.J.: Prentice-Hall, p. 179.

27/6   "imperfect." Friedman, M. with the assistance of Rose
           Friedman. 1963. Capitalism and freedom. Chicago:
           University of Chicago Press, p. 12.

27/15   corporate social responsibility. Ibid., p. 133.

28/2   Coleman, L. 1941. What is American: A study of alleged
           American traits. Social Forces 19: 498.

28/14   "the money medium." Lynd, R. S. and Lynd, H. M. 1929.
           Middletown. New York: Harcourt, Brace, p. 21.

28/21   Thus this crucial activity. Ibid., p. 87.

29/15   Cadman. Abels, J. 1969. In the time of Silent Cal. New
           York: G. P. Putnam's Sons, p. 229.

29/19   Coolidge. Ibid.

29/32   "always moving." Mead, M. 1965. And keep your powder
           dry. New York: William Morrow, p. 39.

29/41   "yearning for achievement." Ibid., p. 113.

30/3   Parenthood in America. Ibid., p. 41.

30/8   Hsu, F. L. K. 1961. American core value and national
           character. In Psychological anthropology. Home-
           wood, Ill.: Dorsey Press.

30/35   McClelland, D. C., Atkinson, J. W., Clark, R. A., and
           Lowell, E. L. 1953. The achievement motive. New
           York: Appleton-Century-Crofts.

31/16   Bronfenbrenner, U. 1970. Two worlds of childhood. New
           York: Simon and Schuster, p. 95.

31/23   consumerism and inflation. Harris, American now, p. 90.

31/32   6% of American families. Ibid., p. 97.

31/36   Bronfenbrenner, op. cit., p. 101.

32/17   Kanter, op. cit., p. 66.

35/1   will of the servant. Fromm, E. and Xirau, R. 1968. The
           nature of man. New York: Macmillan, p. 192.

36/12   Harris, Cannibals, p. 183.

36/25   death rate in England. Ibid., p. 184.

page/line

36/27   increase in crime. Ibid., p. 185.

37/13   "Enthusiasm was general." Giddens, A. 1971. Capitalism and modern social theory. Cambridge, Eng.: Cambridge University Press, p. 3.

37/28   human sensuous activity. Marx, K. and Engels, F. 1976. The German ideology. Moscow: Progress Publishers, p. 616.

38/13   G. Stanley Hall. Bauer, R. A. 1952. The new man in Soviet psychology. Cambridge, Mass.: Harvard University Press, p. 82.

38/18   Marx and Engels, op. cit., pp. 49-50.

38/21   immanent categories. Giddens, op. cit., p. 21.

38/33   ensemble of social relations. Marx and Engels, op. cit., p. 616.

39/7   men lose their personalities. Marx, Early Writings, pp. 350-51.

39/9   bundles of instincts. Marx and Engels, op. cit., p. 50.

39/23   sampling error. Marx, Early Writings, p. 322.

39/30   Marx on Bentham. Marx, K. 1977. Capital I, New York: Vintage, p. 759.

40/5   Robinson Crusoe. Marx, K. 1970. A contribution to the critique of political economy. Moscow: Progress Publishing, p. 188.

40/16   Harris, Cannibals, p. 10.

40/21   competition. Engels, F. 1968. The origin of the family, private property, and the state. In Karl Marx and Frederick Engels: Selected Works. London: Lawrence and Wishart, p. 528.

40/25   pairing family. Ibid., p. 487.

40/40   monogamian society. Ibid., p. 499.

41/5   Engels, F. Ibid., p. 503.

41/15   sexual division of labor. Ibid., p. 580.

41/40   Here a class appears. Ibid., p. 582.

42/14   Smith, op. cit., p. 127.

43/5   Fritzhand, M. 1965. Marx's ideal of man. In Socialist humanism, edited by E. Fromm. Garden City, N.Y.: Doubleday, pp. 157-58.

43/21   Engels, F. 1950. The condition of the working class in England in 1844. London: Allen and Unwin, p. 276.

43/27   Marx, Early Writings, pp. 328-329.

43/33   working conditions. Marx, K. 1977. Capital III. New York: Vintage, pp. 179-180.

43/38   social class and health. Schwab, J. J. and Schwab, M. E.

page/line

1978. Sociocultural roots of mental illness. New York: Plenum, pp. 264-65.

43/45   Hogan, R. 1976. Personality theory. Englewood Cliffs, N.J.: Prentice-Hall, p. 132.

44/37   man is barely human. Marx, Early Writings, p. 349.

45/16   governments as class agents. Marx and Engels, op. cit., pp. 67-71.

47/1   Jung, C. G. 1933. Modern man in search of a soul. New York: Harcourt, Brace and World, p. 40.

47/23   people are basically alike. Roheim, G. 1950. Psychoanalysis and anthropology. New York: International Universities Press.

48/36   Dora. Freud, S. 1963. Dora: An analysis of a case of hysteria. New York: Macmillan.

49/21   symbols. Freud, S. 1938. Psychopathology of everyday life. In The basic writings of Sigmund Freud. New York: Modern Library.

50/33   Hogan, Personality, p. 48.

51/4   Freud, S. 1961. Civilization and its discontents. New York: Norton, p. 58.

51/29   anthropological arguments. Bourgignon, E. 1979. Psychological anthropology. New York: Holt, Rinehart and Winston, pp. 52-53.

51/34   universality of complexes. Ibid., pp. 122-126.

52/10   working hours. Staines, G. L. and Pleck, J. H. 1983. The impact of work schedules on the family. Ann Arbor: Institute for Social Research, p. 17.

52/13   Masnick, G. and Bane, M. J. 1980. The nation's families. Boston: Auburn House, p. 8.

52/19   14% of American families. Levitan, S. A. and Belous, R. S. What's happening to the American family? Baltimore: The Johns Hopkins University Press, p. 8.

52/23   divorce in 1979. Ibid., p. 12.

52/30   Levitan and Belous, op. cit., p. 68.

52/32   earnings of women. Harris, Cannibals, p. 92.

52/34   amount spent on housing. Masnick and Bane, op. cit., p. 105.

52/37   childcare. Ibid., p. 105.

52/39   women in management. Ibid., p. 86.

52/42   percentage of woman managers. Schultz, D. 1982. Psychology and industry today. New York: Macmillan, p. 263.

page/line

53/7   Oedipal victor. Fenichel, O. 1953. Specific forms of the
        Oedipus Complex. In Collected papers of Otto
        Fenichel, First series, edited by H. Fenichel and
        David Rappaport. New York: Norton, p. 213.
53/20   narcissistic mirror. Kohut, H. 1968. The psychoanalytic
        treatment of narcissistic personality disorders. The
        psychoanalytic study of the child, vol. 23. New York:
        International Universities Press, p. 96. Also Blos,
        P. 1962. On adolescence: A psychoanalytic inter-
        pretation. New York: Free Press, p. 235.
53/34   Kerblay, op. cit., p. 124.
53/37   divorce in the USSR. Ibid., p. 124.
53/40   Soviet remarriage. Ibid., p. 126.
54/27   Fromm, E. 1973. The anatomy of human destructiveness.
        New York: Holt, Rinehart and Winston, p. 332.
54/39   Freud and society. Hogan, Personality, pp. 46-52.
56/16   conflict-free sphere. Hartmann, H. 1958. Ego psychology
        and the problem of adaptation. New York: Interna-
        tional Universities Press, pp. 3ff.
56/20   average expectable environment. Ibid., p. 35.
57/20   jettisoned the unpleasant. Marcuse, H. 1962. Eros and
        civilization. New York: Vintage, pp. 215ff.
58/23   Fromm, Beyond the chains.
58/23   Heilbroner, R. 1975. Marxism, psychoanalysis, and the
        problem of a unified theory of behavior. Social
        Research 42: 414-32.
59/1   Skinner, B. F. 1948. Walden two. New York: Macmillan,
        p. 218.
61/18   Skinner, B. F. 1971. Beyond freedom and dignity. 1971.
        New York: Bantam/Vintage, pp. 139-40.
61/41   freedom and dignity. Ibid.
62/16   human conditioning. Bauer, op. cit., p. 54.
62/33   reflex of purpose. Ibid., p. 77.
62/37   Lenin's decree. McLeish, J. 1975. Soviet psychology.
        London: Methuen, p. 151.
63/18   Watson and Raynor. Harris, B. 1979. What ever happened
        to Little Albert? American Psychologist 34: 151.
64/14   Scott Tissue campaign. Lears, T. J. Jackson. 1983. From
        salvation to self-realization. In The culture of con-
        sumption, edited by R. W. Fox and T. J. Jackson
        Lears. New York: Pantheon, p. 24.
64/34   Give me a dozen. Marx, M. H. and Hillix, W. A. Systems
        and theories in psychology. New York: McGraw-Hill,
        p. 185.

page/line

65/34   Kassorla, I. 1974. For catatonia: Smiles, praise, and a
food basket. In Readings in Psychology Today, 3rd.
ed. Del Mar, Calif.: CB, Books.

66/17   New York Herald Tribune. Marx and Hillix, op. cit., p.
200.

66/22   Bandura, A. and Walters, R. H. 1963. Social learning
and personality development. New York: Holt, Rinehart and Winston.

66/30   25 to 30 hours. Fuchs, V. R. 1983. How we live. Cambridge, Mass.: Harvard University Press, p. 55.

66/30   Russian viewing habits. Kerblay, op. cit., p. 141.

66/41   11,000 hours. Rothenberg, M. E. 1975. The effect of
television violence on children and youth. Journal
of the American Medical Association 234: 1043.

67/1   babies' viewing habits. Hollenbeck, A. R. and Slabey,
R. G. 1979. Infant visual and vocal responses to
television. Child Development 50: 44.

67/2   five violent acts. Television and behavior: Ten years of
scientific progress and implications for the eighties,
2 vols. 1982. Rockville, Md.: U.S. Department of
Health and Human Services, Public Health Service,
Alcohol, Drug Abuse, and Mental Health Administration, National Institute of Mental Health, p. 10.

67/5   18,000 murders. Rothenberg, op. cit., p. 1043.

67/10   Television and behavior, vol. 1, p. 6.

67/19   males on television. Ibid., p. 7. Also Barcus, F. E.
1983. Images of life in children's television. New
York: Praeger, p. 59.

67/22   non-working women. Television and behavior, vol. 1,
p. 54. Also Barcus, op. cit., p. 59.

67/26   minorities. Television and behavior, vol. 2, pp. 183-84.

67/32   alcohol. Ibid., vol. 1, p. 11.

67/36   television doctors. Ibid., p. 12.

67/41   22,000 commercials. Ibid., p. 11.

68/20   Barcus, op. cit., p. 13.

68/26   Harris, American now, p. 118.

68/34   Skinner, Beyond freedom, pp. 150-153.

69/42   Aristotle. Ibid., p. 3.

71/11   autonomous man. Ibid., p. 191.

72/17   identify goals. cf. Plamenatz, J. 1975. Karl Marx's
philosophy of man. Oxford: Clarendon Press.

73/1   Lenin. Frolov, I. 1978. Man and his future. World
Marxist Review 21: 119.

page/line

74/21	Pavlik Morozov. Bronfenbrenner, op. cit., p. 47.
75/30	Markarenko. Anton Makarenko: His life and work in education. 1976. Moscow: Progress Publishers, p. 22.
77/6	Clara Zetkin. Rahmani, L. 1973. Soviet psychology. New York: International Universities Press, p. 9.
77/6	Trotsky, op. cit., p. 228.
77/39	chauvinistic opinions. Bauer, op. cit., p. 110.
77/42	test scores of party members. Ibid., p. 113.
78/33	Bronfenbrenner, op. cit., p. 11.
79/2	two months leave. Kerblay, op. cit., p. 151.
79/8	nursery placement. Bronfenbrenner, op. cit., p. 17.
79/13	time off to visit. Kerblay, op. cit., p. 152.
79/19	Ibid., p. 154.
79/40	Hazard, J. N. 1968. The Soviet system of government. Chicago: University of Chicago Press, p. 36.
81/16	Criminal Code of 1919. Bauer, op. cit., p. 41.
81/40	Makarenko. Anton Makarenko, p. 29.
82/13	social mobility. Kerblay, op. cit., p. 155.
82/26	Bronfenbrenner, op. cit., p. 86.
82/37	Andropov. Notable and Quotable, Wall Street Journal, April 14, 1983, p. 28.
83/4	moral code. The road to communism: Documents of the 22nd Congress of the Communist Party of the Soviet Union. 1961. Moscow: Foreign Languages Publishing House, pp. 566–67.
85/1	Reich, W. 1970b. The mass psychology of fascism. New York: Farrar, Straus and Giroux, p. xiii.
86/43	orgastic potency. Reich, W. 1970a. The function of the orgasm. New York: World, p. 360.
87/13	Reich and Freud. Robinson, P. A. 1969. The Freudian left. New York: Harper and Row, pp. 29–30.
88/6	matriarchy. Reich, W. 1976. People in trouble. New York: Farrar, Straus and Giroux, pp. 127–129.
88/27	free love. Kerblay, op. cit., p. 113.
88/29	cult of virginity. Mace, D. and Mace, V. 1963. The Soviet family. London: Hutchinson and Co., p. 72.
88/32	Zetkin. Ibid., pp. 71–72.
88/43	neither monk nor Don Juan. Ibid., p. 73.
89/2	prophylacteria. Ibid., pp. 77–78.
89/8	gonorrhea. Ibid., p. 79.
89/40	Nazi research. Miller, W. W. 1961. Russians as people. New York: Dutton, p. 160.
89/44	first kiss. Mace and Mace, op. cit., p. 81.

page/line

90/4	extramarital sex. Kerblay, op. cit., p. 118.
90/6	illegitimate births. Ibid., p. 119.
90/8	cohabitation. Ibid., p. 119.
90/15	titillation. Mace and Mace, op. cit., p. 80.
91/40	Veblen to Roosevelt. Veblen, T. 1978. The theory of business enterprise. New Brunswick, N.J.: Transaction, p. 398; Also Ginger, op. cit., p. 320.
92/17	May, H. F. 1964. The end of American innocence. Chicago: Quadrangle, p. 180.
92/26	Veblen on Marx. Veblen, T. 1961. The place of science in modern civilization. New York: Russell and Russell, pp. 410-411.
93/22	Pecuniary emulation. Veblen, T. 1953. The theory of the leisure class. New York: New American Library, p. 33ff.
94/1	Goldstein, E. 1979. Psychological adaptations of Soviet immigrants. American Journal of Psychoanalysis 39: 258.
94/21	"force and fraud." Veblen, Leisure class, pp. 152.
95/7	Veblen on leaders. Veblen, T. 1954. Essays in our changing order. New York: Viking, pp. 435-36.
95/38	advertising. Veblen, T. 1967. Absentee ownership. Boston: Beacon, p. 307.
96/2	"arts of business." Ibid., p. 107.
96/24	Bentham. Veblen, Place of science, p. 73.
96/34	totalitarianism. Veblen, Theory of business, pp. 391ff.
96/7	Bolshevik revolution. Veblen, Essays, p. 414.
99/1	Rogers, C. 1974. In retrospect: Forty six years. American Psychologist 29: 121.
102/7	Sartre. Dunayevskaya, R. 1973. Philosophy and revolution. New York: Dell, p. 190.
102/14	a parasitic system. Ibid.
102/44	historical conditions. Marx and Engels, op. cit., p. 2.
104/42	Rogers, C. and Stevens, B. 1967. Person to person. Boulder: Real People Press, pp. 13ff.
105/19	people are good. Ibid., p. 55.
105/28	unconditional positive regard. Rogers, C. R. 1961. On becoming a person. Boston: Houghton-Mifflin, pp. 184-85 and 283-84.
106/9	Maslow, A. 1954. Motivation and personality. New York: Van Nostrand Reinhold.
106/21	self-actualized characteristics. Maslow, A. 1968. Toward a psychology of being, 2nd ed. New York: Van Nostrand Reinhold, p. 26.

page/line

108/3   Soviet study time. Kerblay, op. cit., p. 141.

108/6   "personality market." Fromm, E. 1947. Man for himself. New York: Rinehart, p. 67.

108/17   est self. Bartley, W. W. III. 1978. Werner Erhard. New York: Clarkson N. Potter, p. 181.

108/24   mind vs. self. Ibid., p. 184.

108/38   "positionality." Ibid., p. 174.

109/1   "econiche." Ibid., p. 198.

109/41   Rychlak, J. The psychology of rigorous humanism. New York: Wiley, pp. 496–497.

110/9   Hogan, R. 1983. A socioanalytic theory of personality. In Personality—Current theory and research, edited by M. M. Page. Nebraska Symposium on Motivation. Lincoln: University of Nebraska Press.

111/1   Svitak. Leonhard, W. 1979. Three faces of Marxism. New York: G. P. Putnam's Sons, p. 351.

111/20   Schaff, A. 1965. Marxism and the philosophy of man. In Socialist humanism, edited by E. Fromm. Garden City, N.Y.: Doubleday, p. 134.

112/6   early Marx. Geras, N. 1983. Marx and human nature. London: Verso Editions.

112/6   mature Marx. Althusser, L. 1969. For Marx. New York: Random House.

112/22   Stalin. Leonhard, op. cit., p. 275.

112/39   Marković, M. 1972. Violence and human self–realization. In Essays on socialist humanism, edited by K. Coates. Nottingham, Eng.: The Bertrand Russell Peace Foundation, p. 103.

113/2   Schaff, op. cit., pp. 135–36.

113/25   Marković, M. 1969. Basic characteristics of Marxist humanism. Praxis 3–4: 613.

113/28   his potential powers. Ibid., p. 613.

114/30   Worker Management Councils. Korman, A. K. Organizational behavior. Englewood Cliffs, N.J.: Prentice-Hall, p. 303.

114/43   personal happiness. Leonhard, op. cit., p. 295.

115/2   right of expression. Ibid., p. 295.

115/34   Marcuse, H. 1970. Five lectures: Psychoanalysis, politics, and utopia. Boston: Beacon Press, p. 49.

115/37   Frommian needs. Fromm, E. 1955. The sane society. New York: Rinehart, pp. 27–66.

116/20   Frommian character. Fromm, Man, pp. 62ff.

117/7   sum total of roles. Ibid., p. 72.

page/line

117/34   Reich and Fromm. Reich, Mass psychology, p. 219. Also
          Boadella, D. 1973. Wilhelm Reich: The evolution of
          his work. New York: Dell, pp. 194ff.
118/5   blank sheet of paper. Fromm, Beyond the chains, p. 81.
118/7   social filter. Ibid., p. 121.
118/18   Marcuse, H. 1969. An essay on liberation. Boston:
          Beacon Press, p. 20.
118/24   Stakhanovites. Fainsod, M. 1958. Smolensk under Soviet
          rule. Cambridge, Mass.: Harvard University Press,
          p. 320.
119/6   worker control. Kerblay, op. cit., p. 176.
119/10   criterion for success. Ibid., p. 178.
119/17   turnover. Ibid., p. 190.
119/18   light bulb industry. Yanowitch, M. 1979. Soviet work
          attitudes. White Plains, N.Y.: M. E. Sharpe, p. 19.
119/35   control of supplies. Kerblay, B. Ibid., p. 193.
121/1   Mischel, W. 1979. On the interface of cognition and per-
          sonality. American Psychologist 34: 747.
121/15   Kelly, G. A. 1963. A theory of personality. New York:
          Norton, pp. 4-5.
123/42   templates. Ibid., pp. 8-9.
124/36   Endler, N. S. 1982. Interactionism comes of age. In Con-
          sistency in social behavior: The Ontario Symposium,
          vol. 2, edited by M. P. Zanna, E. T. Higgins, and
          C. P. Herman. Hillsdale, N.J.: p. 230.
125/8   Mischel, op. cit., p. 741.
125/18   anecdotal veto. Bourgignon, op. cit., p. 16.
125/24   "cognitive economics." Mischel, W. 1981. Personality
          and cognition: Something borrowed, something new?
          In Personality, cognition, and social interaction,
          edited by N. Cantor and J. F. Kihlstrom. Hillsdale,
          N.J.: Lawrence Erlbaum, p. 14.
126/5   "consensual prototypes." Cantor, N. 1981. A cognitive-
          social approach to personality. In Personality, cog-
          nition, and social interaction, edited by N. Cantor
          and J. F. Kihlstrom. Hillsdale, N.J.: Lawrence
          Erlbaum, p. 28.
126/7   "interaction competencies." Athay, M. and Darling, J. M.
          1981. Toward an interaction-centered theory of per-
          sonality. In Personality, cognition, and social inter-
          action, edited by N. Cantor and J. F. Kihlstrom.
          Hillsdale, N.J.: Lawrence Erlbaum, p. 299.
126/8   "other person categories." Cantor, op. cit., p. 31.

page/line

126/23   Paivio. Rogers, T. B. 1981. A model of the self as an
          aspect of the human information processing system.
          In Personality, cognition, and social interaction,
          edited by N. Cantor and J. F. Kihlstrom. Hillsdale,
          N.J.: Lawrence Erlbaum, p. 211.
126/39   individuality. Mischel, op. cit., p. 740.
127/2   Myasischev. Ziferstein, I. 1983. Soviet personality theory.
          In Personality theories, research and assessment,
          edited by R. J. Corsini and A. J. Marsella. Itasca,
          Ill.: F. E. Peacock, p. 525.
127/34   defining a situation. Stebbins, R. A. 1972. Studying the
          definition of the situation: Theory and field research
          strategies. In Symbolic interaction, 2nd ed., edited
          by J. G. Manis and B. N. Meltzer. Boston: Allyn
          and Bacon.
127/44   Trotsky. Dunayevskaya, op. cit., p. xviii.
128/1   Smirnov, A. A. 1973. The development of Soviet psy-
          chology. In Soviet psychology: A symposium.
          Westport, Conn.: Greenwood Press, pp. 22-24.
128/11   Lenin. Dunayevskaya, op. cit., p. 98.
129/18   Krutetski. Ziferstein, op. cit., p. 573.
129/35   Ziferstein, op. cit., p. 496.
130/15   Andropov. Notable & Quotable. Wall Street Journal, April
          14, 1983, p. 28.
131/1   Dewey, J. 1927. The public and its problems. New York:
          Henry Holt, p. 33.
131/10   Bock, P. K. 1980. Continuities in psychological anthro-
          pology. San Francisco: W. H. Freeman, pp. 185-
          204.
132/42   Reich, People, pp. 6ff.
135/30   Soviet Constitution. Strong, A. L. 1937. The new Soviet
          constitution. New York: Henry Holt, pp. 152ff.

Bibliography

Abels, J. 1969. In the time of Silent Cal. New York: G. P. Putnam's
    Sons.

Allport, G. 1961. Pattern and growth in personality. New York: Holt,
    Rinehart and Winston.

Althusser, L. 1969. For Marx. New York: Random House.

Anton Makarenko: His life and work in education. 1976. Moscow:
    Progress Publishers.

Athay, M., and Darley, J. M. 1981. Toward an interaction-centered
    theory of personality. In Personality, cognition, and social in-
    teraction, edited by N. Cantor and J. F. Kihlstrom. Hillsdale,
    N.J.: Lawrence Erlbaum.

Bandura, A., and Walters, R. H. 1963. Social learning and person-
    ality development. New York: Holt, Rinehart and Winston.

Barcus, F. E. 1983. Images of life in children's television. New
    York: Praeger.

Bartley, W. W. III. 1978. Werner Erhard. New York: Clarkson N.
    Potter.

Barton, B. 1962. The man nobody knows. Indianapolis: Bobbs-Merrill.

Bauer, R. A. 1952. The new man in Soviet psychology. Cambridge,
    Mass.: Harvard University Press.

Blos, P. 1962. On adolesence: A psychoanalytic interpretation. New
    York: Free Press.

Blumenstein, P., and Schwartz, P. 1983. American couples. New
    York: William Morrow.

Boadella, D. 1973. Wilhelm Reich: The evolution of his work. New
    York: Dell.

Bock, P. K. 1980. Continuities in psychological anthropology. San Francisco, W. H. Freeman.

Bourgignon, E. 1979. Psychological anthropology. New York: Holt, Rinehart and Winston.

Bramel, D., and Friend, R. 1981. Hawthorne, the myth of the docile worker, and class bias in psychology. American Psychologist 36: 867-78.

Brigham, J. C. 1971. Ethnic stereotypes. Psychological Bulletin 76: 15-38.

Bronfenbrenner, J. 1970. Two worlds of childhood. New York: Simon and Schuster.

Bruner, E. M. 1956. Primary group experience and the process of acculturation. American Anthropologist 58: 605-23.

Cantor, N. 1981. A cognitive-social approach to personality. In Personality, cognition, and social interaction, edited by N. Cantor and J. F. Kihlstrom. Hillsdale, N.J.: Lawrence Erlbaum.

Coleman, L. 1941. What is American: A study of alleged American traits. Social Forces 19: 498.

Dewey, J. 1927. The public and its problems. New York: Henry Holt.

Dobriansky, L. E. 1957. Veblenism: A new critique. Washington, DC.: Public Affairs Press.

Dorfman, J. 1961. Thorstein Veblen and his America. New York: Augustus M. Kelley.

Dowd, D. 1966. Thorstein Veblen. New York: Washington Square Press.

Dunayevskaya, R. 1973. Philosophy and revolution. New York: Dell.

Endler, N. S. 1982. Interactionism comes of age. In Consistency in social behavior: The Ontario Symposium, vol. 2, edited by M. P. Zanna, E. T. Higgins, and C. P. Herman. Hillsdale, N.J.: Lawrence Erlbaum.

Engels, F. 1968. The origin of the family, private property and the state. In Karl Marx and Frederick Engels: Selected Works. London: Lawrence and Wishart.

_____. 1950. The condition of the working class in England in 1844. London: Allen and Unwin.

Erikson, E. 1963. Childhood and society, 2nd ed. New York: W. W. Norton.

Fainsod, M. 1958. Smolensk under Soviet rule. Cambridge, Mass.: Harvard University Press.

Fenichel, O. 1953. Specific forms of the Oedipus Complex. In Collected Papers of Otto Fenichel, First series, edited by H. Fenichel and David Rappaport. New York: W. W. Norton.

Freud, S. 1959. Beyond the pleasure principle. New York: Bantam.

_____. 1961. Civilization and its discontents. New York: Norton.

_____. 1963. Dora: An analysis of a case of hysteria. New York: Macmillan.

_____. 1959. Group psychology and the analysis of the ego. New York: Norton.

_____. 1938a. Psychopathology of everyday life. In The basic writings of Sigmund Freud, edited by A. A. Brill. New York: Modern Library.

_____. 1938b. Totem and taboo. In The basic writings of Sigmund Freud, edited by A. A. Brill. New York: Modern Library.

_____. 1918. Reflections on war and death. New York: Moffat, Yard.

Friedman, M. 1975. An economist's protest, 2nd ed. Glen Ridge, N.J.: Thomas Horton.

Friedman, M., and Friedman, R. 1980. Free to choose. New York: Harcourt Brace Jovanovich.

Friedman, M., with the assistance of Rose Friedman. 1963. Capitalism and freedom. Chicago: University of Chicago Press.

Fritzhand, M. 1965. Marx's ideal of man. In Socialist humanism, edited by E. Fromm. Garden City, N.Y.: Doubleday.

Frolov, I. 1978. Man and his future. World Marxist Review 21:115-25.

Fromm, E. 1976. To have or to be? New York: Harper and Row.

_____. 1973. The anatomy of human destructiveness. New York: Holt, Rinehart and Winston.

_____. 1962. Beyond the chains of illusion. New York: Simon and Schuster.

_____. 1961. Marx's concept of man. New York: Frederick Ungar.

_____. 1955. The sane society. New York: Rinehart.

_____. 1947. Man for himself. New York: Rinehart.

Fromm, E. and Xirau, R. 1968. The nature of man. New York: Macmillan.

Fuchs, V. R. 1983. How we live. Cambridge, Mass.: Harvard University Press.

Geras, N. 1983. Marx and human nature. London: Verso Editions.

Giddens, A. 1971. Capitalism and modern social theory. Cambridge, England: Cambridge University Press.

Gilder, G. 1981. Wealth and poverty. New York: Basic Books.

Ginger, R. 1965. Age of excess. New York: Macmillan.

Goldstein, E. 1979. Psychological adaptations of Soviet immigrants. American Journal of Psychoanalysis 39: 257-63.

Harris, B. 1979. What ever happened to Little Albert? American Psychologist 34: 151-60.

_____. 1981. America now. New York: Simon and Schuster.

_____. 1979. Cultural materialism. New York: Random House.

Harris, M. 1977. Cannibals and kings. New York: Random House.

Hartmann, H. 1958. Ego psychology and the problem of adaptation. New York: International Universities Press.

Hazard, J. N. 1968. The Soviet system of government, 4th ed. Chicago: University of Chicago Press.

Heilbroner, R. 1975. Marxism, psychoanalysis, and the problem of a unified theory of behavior. Social Research 42: 414-32.

Hofstadter, R. 1955. Social Darwinism in American thought. Boston: Beacon Press.

Hogan, R. 1983. A socioanalytic theory of personality. In Personality—Current theory and research, edited by M. M. Page. Nebraska Symposium on Motivation. Lincoln: University of Nebraska Press.

_____. 1976. Personality theory. Englewood Cliffs, N.J.: Prentice-Hall.

Holland, J. L. 1979. The Self-Directed Search Professional Manual. Palo Alto, Ca.: Consulting Psychologists Press.

_____. 1966. The psychology of vocational choice: A theory of personality types and model environments. Waltham, Mass.: Blaisdell.

Hollenbeck, A. R., and Slabey, R. G. 1979. Infant visual and vocal responses to television. Child Development 50: 41-45.

Hsu, F. L. K. 1983. Rugged individualism reconsidered. Knoxville: University of Tennessee Press.

_____. 1961. American core value and national character. In Psychological Anthropology. Homewood, Ill.: Dorsey Press.

Inkeles, A., Hanfmann, E., and Beier, H. 1958. Modal personality and adjustment to the Soviet sociopolitical system. Human Relations 11: 3-22.

Jung, C. G. 1933. Modern man in search of a soul. New York: Harcourt, Brace, and World.

Kanter, R. M. 1977. Men and women of the corporation. New York: Basic Books.

Kassorla, I. 1974. For catatonia: Smiles, praise, and a food basket. In Readings in Psychology Today, 3rd ed. Del Mar, Calif.: CRM Books.

Katona, G. 1980. Essays on behavioral economics. Ann Arbor: University of Michigan Press.

_____. 1963. Psychological analysis of economic behavior. New York: McGraw-Hill.

_____. 1963a. The relationship between psychology and economics. In Psychology: The study of a science, vol. 6, edited by Sigmund Koch. New York: McGraw-Hill.

Kelly, G. A. 1963. A theory of personality. New York: Norton.

Kerblay, B. 1983. Modern Soviet society. New York: Pantheon Books.

Kohut, H. 1968. The psychoanalytic treatment of narcissistic personality disorders. The Psychoanalytic Study of the Child, vol. 23. New York: International Universities Press.

Korman, A. K. 1977. Organizational behavior. Englewood Cliffs, N.J.: Prentice-Hall.

Lears, T. J. Jackson. 1983. From salvation to self-realization. In The culture of consumption, edited by R. W. Fox and T. J. Jackson Lears. New York: Pantheon.

Leonhard, W. 1979. Three faces of Marxism. New York: G. P. Putnam's Sons.

Levitan, S. A. and Belous, R. S. 1981. What's happening to the American family? Baltimore: The Johns Hopkins University Press.

Lynd, R. S. and Lynd, H. M. 1929. Middletown. New York: Harcourt, Brace.

Mace, D., and Mace, V. 1963. The Soviet family. London: Hutchinson and Co.

Mandel, E., and Novak, G. 1970. The Marxist theory of alienation. New York: Pathfinder.

Marcuse, H. 1970. Five lectures: Psychoanalysis, politics, and utopia. Boston: Beacon Press.

_____. 1969. An essay on liberation. Boston: Beacon Press.

_____. 1965. Socialist humanism? In Socialist humanism, edited by E. Fromm. Garden City, N.Y.: Doubleday.

_____. 1962. Eros and civilization. New York: Vintage.

Marković, M. 1972. Violence and human self-realisation. In Essays on socialist humanism, edited by K. Coates. Nottingham, England: The Bertrand Russell Peace Foundation.

_____. 1969. Basic characteristics of Marxist humanism. Praxis 3-4: 606-15.

Marx, K. 1975. Economic and Philosophic Manuscripts of 1844. In Early Writings. New York: Vintage.

_____. 1977. Capital I. New York: Vintage.

_____. 1977. Capital III. New York: Vintage.

_____. 1970. A contribution to the critique of political economy. Moscow: Progress Publishers.

Marx, K., and Engels, F. 1976. The German ideology. Moscow: Progress Publishers.

Marx, M. H., and Hillix, W. A. 1973. Systems and theories in psychology. New York: McGraw-Hill.

Maslow, A. Motivation and personality. 1954. New York: Van Nostrand Rheinhold.

_____. 1968. Toward a psychology of being, 2nd ed. New York: Van Nostrand Reinhold.

Masnick, G., and Bane, M. J. 1980. The nation's families: 1960-1990. Boston: Auburn House.

May, H. F. 1964. The end of American innocence. Chicago: Quadrangle.

McClelland, D. C., Atkinson, J. W., Clark, R. A., and Lowell, E. L. 1953. The achievement motive. New York: Appleton-Century-Crofts.

McLeish, J. 1975. Soviet psychology. London: Metheun.

Mead, M. 1965. And keep your powder dry. New York: William Morrow.

Miller, W. W. 1961. Russians as people. New York: Dutton.

Mischel, W. 1981. Personality and cognition: Something borrowed, something new? In Personality, cognition, and social interaction, edited by N. Cantor and J. F. Kihlstrom. Hillsdale, N.J.: Lawrence Erlbaum.

_____. 1979. On the interface of cognition and personality. American Psychologist 34: 740-54.

Mischel, W., and Peake, P. 1982. In search of consistency: Measure for measure. In Consistency in social behavior: The Ontario Symposium, vol. 2, edited by M. P. Zanna, E. T. Higgins, and C. P. Herman. Hillsdale, N.J.: Lawrence Erlbaum.

Mitzman, Arthur. 1973. Sociology and estrangement. New York: Knopf.

Moore, W. 1962. The conduct of the corporation. New York: Random House.

Neubauer, P. B. 1972. Psychoanalysis of the preschool child. In Handbook of child psychoanalysis, edited by B. B. Wolman. New York: Van Nostrand Reinhold.

_____. 1960. The one-parent child and his oedipal development. Psychoanalytic Study of the Child. New York: International Universities Press.

Ouspensky, P. D. 1971. The fourth way. New York: Vintage Books.

Payne, T. R. 1968. S. L. Rubinshtein and the philosophical foundation of Soviet psychology. Dordecht, Holland: D. Reidel.

Plamenatz, J. 1975. Karl Marx's philosophy of man. Oxford: Clarendon Press.

Rahmani, L. 1973. Soviet psychology. New York: International Universities Press.

Reich, W. 1976. People in trouble. New York: Farrar, Straus, and Giroux.

_____. 1974. The sexual revolution. New York: Simon and Schuster.

_____. 1972. Character analysis. New York: Simon and Schuster.

_____. 1970a. The function of the orgasm. New York: World.

_____. 1970b. The mass psychology of facism. New York: Farrar, Straus and Giroux.

The road to communism: Documents of the 22nd Congress of the Communist Party of the Soviet Union. 1961. Moscow: Foreign Languages Publishing House.

Robertson, H. M. 1959. A criticism of Max Weber and his school. In Protestantism and capitalism: The Weber thesis and its critics, edited by Robert W. Green. Lexington, Mass.: D. C. Heath.

Robinson, D. N. 1982. Toward a science of human nature. New York: Columbia University Press.

Robinson, P. A. 1969. The Freudian left. New York: Harper and Row.

Roethlisberger, F. J., and Dickson, W. J. 1939. Management and the worker. New York: Wiley.

Rogers, C. R. 1974. In retrospect: Forty six years. American Psychologist 29: 115–23.

_____. 1961. On becoming a person. Boston: Houghton Mifflin.

Rogers, C. R., and Stevens, B. 1967. Person to person. Boulder: Real People Press.

Rogers, T. B. 1981. A model of the self as an aspect of the human information processing system. In Personality, cognition, and social interaction, edited by N. Cantor and J. F. Kihlstrom. Hillsdale, N.J.: Lawrence Erlbaum.

Roheim, G. 1950. Psychoanalysis and anthropology. New York: International Universities Press.

Rothenberg, M. E. 1975. The effect of television violence on children and youth. Journal of the American Medical Association 234: 1,043–46.

Rychlak, J. 1977. The psychology of rigorous humanism. New York: Wiley.

Schaff, A. 1970. Marxism and the individual. Robert S. Cohen, ed. New York: McGraw-Hill.

_____. 1965. Marxism and the philosophy of man. In Socialist human-ism, edited by E. Fromm. Garden City, N. Y.: Doubleday.

Schultz, D. 1982. Psychology and industry today. New York: Mac-millan.

Schwab, J. J., and Schwab, M. E. 1978. Sociocultural roots of mental illness. New York: Plenum.

Skinner, B. F. 1971. Beyond freedom and dignity. New York: Bantam/ Vintage.

_____. 1948. Walden Two. New York: Macmillan.

Smirnov, A. A. 1973. The development of Soviet psychology. In Soviet Psychology: A Symposium. Westport, Conn.: Greenwood Press.

Smith, A. 1937. An inquiry into the nature and causes of the wealth of nations. New York: Random House.

Smither, R. 1982. Human migration and the acculturation of minori-ties. Human Relations 35: 57-68.

Sombart, W. 1982. The Jews and modern capitalism. New Brunswick, N.J.: Transaction Books.

_____. 1967. The quintessence of capitalism. New York: Howard Fertig.

Spindler, G. and L. 1983. Anthropologists view American culture. In Annual Review of Anthropology, edited by B. J. Siegel, A. R. Beals, S. A. Tyler. Palo Alto, Ca.: Annual Reviews.

Staines, G. L., and Pleck, J. H. 1983. The impact of work schedules on the family. Ann Arbor: Institute for Social Research.

Stebbins, R. A. 1972. Studying the definition of the situation: Theory and field research strategies. In Symbolic interaction, 2nd ed., edited by J. G. Manis and B. N. Meltzer. Boston: Allyn and Bacon.

Strong, A. L. 1937. The new Soviet constitution. New York: Henry Holt.

Sumner, W. G. 1963. The absurd effort to make the world over. In Social Darwinism. Englewood Cliffs, N.J.: Prentice-Hall.

Tawney, R. H. 1959. Religion and the rise of capitalism. In Protestantism and capitalism: The Weber thesis and its critics, edited by Robert W. Green. Lexington, Mass.: D. C. Heath.

Television and behavior: Ten years of scientific progress and implications for the eighties, 2 vols. 1982. Rockville, Md.: U.S. Department of Health and Human Services, Public Health Service, Alcohol, Drug Abuse, and Mental Health Administration, National Institute of Mental Health.

Troeltsch, E. 1959. The economic ethic of Calvinism. In Protestantism and capitalism: The Weber Thesis and its critics, edited by R. W. Green. Lexington, Mass.: D. C. Heath.

Trotsky, L. 1975. My life. Middlesex, Eng.: Penguin.

Veblen, T. 1978. The theory of business enterprise. New Brunswick, N.J.: Transaction.

_____. 1967. Absentee ownership. Boston: Beacon.

_____. 1961. The place of science in modern civilization. New York: Russell and Russell.

_____. 1954. Essays in our changing order. New York: Viking.

_____. 1953. The theory of the leisure class. New York: New American Library.

_____. 1914. The instinct of workmanship. New York: Macmillan.

Venable, V. 1945. Human nature: The Marxian view. New York: Knopf.

Wall Street Journal, Labor Letter, November 8, 1983, p. 1.

Wall Street Journal, April 14, 1983, p. 28.

Weber, M. 1958. The Protestant ethic and the spirit of capitalism. New York: Charles Scribner's Sons.

White, L. 1975. The concept of cultural systems. New York: Columbia University Press.

Wilhite, V. G. 1958. Founders of American economic thought and policy. New York: Bookman Associates.

Wilson, E. 1940. To the Finland station. Garden City: Doubleday.

Wolfenstein, E. V. 1967. The revolutionary personality. Princeton, N.J.: Princeton University Press.

Yanowitch, M. 1979. Soviet work attitudes. White Plains, N.Y.: M. E. Sharpe.

Ziferstein, I. 1983. Soviet personality theory. In Personality theories, research, and assessment, edited by Corsini, R. J., and A. J. Marsella. Itasca, Illinois: F. E. Peacock.

Index

About the Author

ROBERT D. SMITHER is an industrial/organizational psychologist at HSI, Inc., a management consulting firm in Washington, D.C. Dr. Smither also teaches in the psychology department at Georgetown University.

Dr. Smither has published widely in the areas of minority acculturation, personality theory and assessment, and vocational behavior. He is currently working on a book about organizational psychology.

Dr. Smither holds a B.A. from Indiana University in political science and a Ph.D. in psychology from The Johns Hopkins University.

DATE DUE

APR 2 6 1989			
FEB 2 4 1996			